M000236083

Fans

ALSO BY MICHAEL BOND

Way Out West
The Power of Others
Wayfinding

Fans

A Journey into the
Psychology of Belonging

MICHAEL BOND

PICADOR

First published 2023 by Picador
an imprint of Pan Macmillan
The Smithson, 6 Briset Street, London ECIM 5NR
EU representative: Macmillan Publishers Ireland Ltd, 1st Floor, The Liffey Trust Centre,
117–126 Sheriff Street Upper, Dublin 1, DOI YC43
Associated companies throughout the world
www.panmacmillan.com

ISBN 978-1-5290-5247-3

Copyright © Michael Bond 2023

The right of Michael Bond to be identified as the
author of this work has been asserted by him in accordance
with the Copyright, Designs and Patents Act 1988.

All rights reserved. No part of this publication may be reproduced,
stored in a retrieval system, or transmitted, in any form, or by any means
(electronic, mechanical, photocopying, recording or otherwise)
without the prior written permission of the publisher.

Pan Macmillan does not have any control over, or any responsibility for,
any author or third-party websites referred to in or on this book.

1 3 5 7 9 8 6 4 2

A CIP catalogue record for this book is available from the British Library.

Typeset in Dante MT Std by Palimpsest Book Production Ltd, Falkirk, Stirlingshire

Printed and bound by CPI Group (UK) Ltd, Croydon, CR0 4YY

This book is sold subject to the condition that it shall not, by way of
trade or otherwise, be lent, hired out, or otherwise circulated without
the publisher's prior consent in any form of binding or cover other than
that in which it is published and without a similar condition including
this condition being imposed on the subsequent purchaser.

Visit **www.picador.com** to read more about all our books
and to buy them. You will also find features, author interviews and
news of any author events, and you can sign up for e-newsletters
so that you're always first to hear about our new releases.

For all fans everywhere who have suffered for their passions

Contents

I

A Social History of Fandoms

I USED TO SPEND MY days in a library in central London,[1] and occasionally on my walk there from the bus stop I would find myself having to negotiate a queue of hundreds of excited children that began at the doors of the flagship branch of Waterstone's bookshop on Piccadilly and continued around the block onto Jermyn Street and down the hill into St James's Square. Many of them were dressed as characters from the netherworld, and they behaved as if something was about to happen that would change their lives for ever. And so it did. A few hours later, they shuffled up the street and into the shop and became some of the first young people in the world to get their hands on a copy of the latest Harry Potter book.

J. K. Rowling's boy wizard wasn't the first imaginary hero to draw big crowds. Nearly two centuries ago, lovers of Charles Dickens's serialized fiction queued for hours at kiosks and lending libraries to buy or borrow the latest instalment and turned up in their thousands to hear him read in public. After the success of *The Pickwick Papers*, the last part of which sold a remarkable 40,000 copies, Dickens became a literary celebrity, perhaps the first of his kind. 'To walk with him in the streets of London was a revelation; a royal progress; people of all degrees and classes taking off their hats and greeting him as he passed,' his son Henry recollected in 1928.[2] A few decades later, the reading public showed a comparable level of affection for Arthur Conan Doyle and his Sherlock Holmes stories.[3] 'The scenes at the railway-bookstalls were worse than anything I ever saw at a bargain-sale,' reported one witness.[4]

Like those young readers who queued for Harry Potter, aficionados of Dickens and of Doyle were 'fans' by any modern definition of the word, though in their time they would not have been categorized that way. The word did not come into regular use until the first decade of the twentieth century; derived from 'fanatic', it was coined in 1884 by the baseball promoter Ted Sullivan to describe the devoted patrons of his sport.[5] 'The baseball fan is an unique American species and the most rabid of all enthusiasts,' noted *The American Magazine* in 1910. 'Compared with him the golf fan, the bridge fan, even the bowling fan are mild.'[6]

Fannish devotion is a gregarious impulse. It is possible to be a solitary fan and to worship from afar, but at some point most of us want to vent our passions with others, to pay homage with fellow enthusiasts. 'If you love something that much, you want to share it, you want to reach out to other people and talk about it,' says Kathy Larsen, who studies fan cultures at George Washington University.

Reaching out to other people who share an interest has not always been easy. In the nineteenth and early twentieth centuries, fans would have struggled to meet people beyond their immediate neighbourhoods (though sports fans could scratch that itch simply by turning up to a game). Then, in 1926, an American publisher called Hugo Gernsback launched *Amazing Stories*, a monthly magazine dedicated to science fiction. The revolution that transformed the social life of fans began, improbably, on its letters page. The magazine adopted the unusual policy of printing the postal addresses of its correspondents, which allowed them to write to each other. Its readers began to realize that there were other people out there who loved what they loved, and they very much wanted to find them. Some of them became pen-pals, formed fan clubs and published magazines – or 'fanzines' – of their own. They were arguably the first ever dedicated fan communities, and almost certainly the first known science-fiction fandoms.[7]

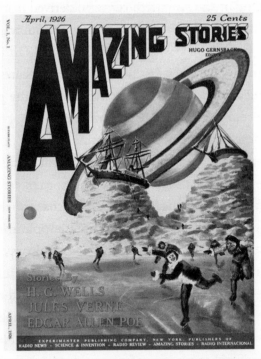

Amazing Stories paved the way for the first science-fiction fandoms by printing contributors' addresses on its letters page.

By the 1960s, science-fiction fans had become advocates and agitators as well as consumers. When NBC threatened to cancel *Star Trek* in 1967 after just two seasons, its producers received 115,893 letters demanding that it continue (they duly obliged).[8] By 1988, at least 120 fan-produced *Star Trek* magazines were in circulation.[9] Despite the show's popularity, its fan following was little more than a cult phenomenon compared with what was to come. *Star Wars*, which began in 1977, took fan participation to another level. Its fandom became a global movement. 'For many people, including me, it is the single most important cultural text of our lives,' wrote the media studies expert Will Brooker in 2002.[10] Heartfelt declarations of commitment to this franchise became a regular part of mainstream culture – such as this one, from a 2013 survey of a *Star Wars* online community:

> Aside from biological imperatives and overall cultural factors, there is nothing that has influenced me, coloured my perception of reality, or shaped my approach to life as much as *Star Wars*. If you cut me open, I bleed *Star Wars*.[11]

———

In the days before social media, establishing a social scene around your passions required considerable ingenuity and persistence. Leah Holmes, who studies the culture and history of Japanese animation (or animé) at Bath Spa University, remembers feeling 'very lonely' growing up in a small town in Ireland in the 1980s and 1990s with no one around to share her love of Japanese comic books and videos. We chatted in March 2020 at Minami Con, one of the last fan conventions before the UK shut down in the early days of the coronavirus pandemic. Later that day she would be speaking on a panel in front of hundreds of other animé fans, a set of circumstances that would have seemed extraordinary to her thirty years ago when her fannish activities barely extended beyond her bedroom.

Leah's initiation into organized fandom happened after she bought a copy of a new animé magazine and spotted a notice about an all-female fan club called Animé Babes. She signed up and was surprised to learn that the club was run by teenagers like herself. They were endeavouring to create a space for female fans of Japanese animé in a market that was geared almost entirely towards men. One of the founders, Lisa-Jane Holmes (no relation to Leah), told me via email that they wanted to show the genre had much to offer beyond the sex and violence that featured in most UK releases. 'There were stories about female superheroes, crime-fighting female cops, stories about female friendship, plenty of beautiful romantic series about love and relationships – and yet animé culture had this stigma that it was giant robots and tentacle pornography, catering for geeky boys sat alone in their bedrooms.'

It cost £1.50 to join Animé Babes. That bought you a quarterly fanzine and – even more appealing to bedroom fans – a list of members' names and addresses, which made it easy to trade tapes, merchandise and letters. 'It was such an important part of my teenage years, especially as it put me in touch with other girls,' said Leah. 'I was used to the things I was interested in being dominated by men.' Since then, the demographics of the fanbase have changed significantly. In 2017, Leah conducted a study of animé fans in the UK and found that more than half of them were female. 'If the members of Animé Babes had known that this was where we'd end up, we'd have been really proud.'[12]

The internet has not radically altered the nature of people's relationships with their heroes or the objects of their passion

Animé Babes was the first fanzine for women in a market
that was dominated by men. (Laura Watton)

– what it *feels* like to be a fan – even though social media has
made celebrities appear more accessible. Fans of Billie Holiday
in the 1940s were no less emotional and committed than fans of
Billie Eilish are today. Even before the invention of the word
'fan', young city-dwellers in the US flocked to concert halls with
a zeal that alarmed their elders. 'Fandom is often characterized
in media studies as a product of mass consumer culture in the
twentieth century,' notes the cultural historian Daniel Cavicchi,
who spent several years studying the diaries, scrapbooks and
letters of music-lovers of the nineteenth century. Yet 'the basic
practices associated with fandom – idealized connection with a

star, strong feelings of memory and nostalgia, use of collecting to develop a sense of self, for example – precede the development of electronic "mass communication" technologies.'[13]

Without doubt, the internet *has* profoundly changed the dynamics of fan communities and the ability of fans to access them. 'Before, everything was done through the mail and it was a really slow and sort of disjointed process, and unless you were living someplace there was a fan community you were pretty cut off and probably felt a bit weird,' says Kathy Larsen, who is proud to consider herself a 'fangirl' as well as a university professor. 'Once everyone got online, it became immediate, and those bonds between fans became far stronger than they had been. And if you want to find someone else who is a fan of some obscure television show, you can guarantee you're going to find a friendly community somewhere online.'

Social media has made it possible for communities to flourish where none existed, among people who because of embarrassment or geography were previously unable to reach out. It has also enabled something more subversive and perhaps more sinister: the migration of fan sensibilities into politics. The relationship between political leaders and their supporters increasingly resembles the relationship between celebrities and their fan groups. This may be true on a cognitive level. In a study published in 2018, researchers at Virginia Tech University found that sports fans and political supporters process new information about their team or party in much the same way, by filtering it through the lens of group affiliation. What matters to people is not the information itself so much as the way it reflects on their group. Fans have always shown a dogged and sometimes irrational allegiance to their tribe, a trait that has become endemic in party politics.[14]

In this pop-culture milieu, political parties are like personality cults, and their leaders are symbolic of their group's identity. So in addition to Janeites (fans of Jane Austen), Beliebers (Justin Bieber) and Swifties (Taylor Swift), we now have MAGAs (Donald Trump), Corbynistas (Jeremy Corbyn) and Boristas (Boris Johnson). In the UK, we also have Brexiteers and Remainers, who embrace their ideologies with a similar level of zeal. In line with their celebrity status, it has become customary for politicians to emphasize performance and personality over policies, and their audiences are happy to play along. Sometimes they make the running for them. When anti-government protestors in Thailand rallied in the streets in August 2020 to demand a new constitution and limits to the power of the monarchy, many of them waved wands or dressed as characters from Hogwarts to symbolize their fight against injustice and autocracy.

Focusing on aesthetics, or on a charismatic figure who appears to personify our cultural group, can make politics more accessible. But it can also cause us to take our eyes off the things that really matter, such as ideas and policies, and to fail to hold our leaders to account. One of the curious things about the Partygate scandal was that Boris Johnson managed to retain so much support even after he had lost the moral argument. So long as our guy is ahead, do we care what they actually do?

———

The convergence of politics and fandom has happened at many points in history. In post-Revolutionary France, Napoleon Bonaparte managed to raise a citizen army – a 'fan army' as it is sometimes called – through the force of his popularity and an appeal to his people's patriotism.[15] Lately, public life and fandom have become ever more entwined. Social media has enabled people who have common interests to participate and cooperate on a scale that was not previously possible. Fans today have unprecedented levels of power. They are so well connected, so quick to mobilize and so much part of the mainstream that politicians, businesses and media producers go out of their way to court them and find out what they think. They have become too consequential and too numerous to ignore.

Like popular social movements, fandoms are places of revolution. The forces at play can change the lives of individuals, and they can also change the world. On 8 October 2018, Taylor Swift broke her self-imposed silence on all things political when she urged her followers to vote in the US mid-term elections and endorsed two Democratic candidates for the Senate and the House of Representatives in her home state of Tennessee. 'So many intelligent, thoughtful, self-possessed people have turned 18 in the past two years and now have the right and privilege to make their vote count,' she wrote on her Instagram, before explaining that in order to vote they first needed to register. Swift's chosen candidate for Senate didn't win, but in the twenty-four hours following her intervention there was a huge spike in the number of people registering to vote nationwide. The largest increases were in the eighteen-to-twenty-nine age group, the demographic of her fanbase. Her fans may not have succeeded in changing the world, but they showed how it might be done.[16]

If you're in any doubt about the ability of fan communities to pull together for a common goal, you need look only to K-pop. In 2020, after George Floyd was killed by a police officer in Minneapolis, tens of thousands of fans of BTS and other South Korean pop bands used their online savvy to block anti-protest surveillance apps, derail racist Twitter campaigns and raise money for Black Lives Matter. K-pop fans do not all speak with one voice – the fandom is as disparate in its views as any community – but they are quick to mobilize. The social justice actions were incredibly effective. When #whitelivesmatter began trending on Twitter as part of a pushback among white conservatives, fans hijacked the hashtag by flooding it with videos of their favourite artist, and before long anyone searching for #whitelivesmatter would see only K-pop stars gyrating or performing pelvic thrusts onstage.

In the modern culture, fandoms are the new tribes. They are subcultures with their own values, vocabularies and aspirations. They attract people with widely divergent experiences and backgrounds: when you love something that other people love, many of the traditional social boundaries fall away. We join them not so much to be entertained as to experience a particular reality, to broaden our perspective, to connect with like-minded others or to find meaning in life. This is not so different to why people participate in a religion, sign up to a political party or even join the army. Fandoms have all the power and influence of those institutions, and they are driven by the same fundamental psycho-social forces.

––––––

Fans is partly about the impact that fandoms have on our culture, but mostly it is about the impact they have on the people who belong to them. Almost all of us, at some point in our lives, become a fan of something. Every cultural phenomenon – TV show, film franchise, sci-fi classic, literary hero, historical icon, comic strip, pop group, celebrity brand or sports team – has its devoted followers. As we'll discover, fans exist in places you would never think of looking. Some of Jane Austen's most loyal followers are twenty-something feminists. Richard III, the 'Hunchback King' who supposedly killed his nephews in the Tower of London, is today defended by a group of amateur historians convinced that his reputation has been traduced. In the US and Britain, thousands of middle-aged men who call themselves 'Bronies' gather in online communities to celebrate the characters in the children's toy line My Little Pony. One of the subcultures that has been most extensively studied by psychologists consists of people who feel a strong affection for anthropomorphic animals. There is also a group of people who believe with complete sincerity that they are animals trapped in a human body.

This book is a story of what happens to us when we interact with people who share our passions. We'll be travelling through a constellation of fandoms, and along the way I hope to demonstrate some fundamental truths about the human condition. The human brain is wired to reach out. While those groupish tendencies can bring much strife, they are also the source of some of our greatest satisfactions. Fandoms offer the pleasures of tribalism with less of the harm: a feeling of belonging and shared culture, a sense of significance and purpose, improved mental well-being, reassurance that your most outlandish convictions will be taken seriously and the freedom to emulate (and dress like) your heroes.

In Chapter 2, we will look at one of the fundamental drivers of these dynamics: group identity. Like it or not, we all strive to classify ourselves with others, even if we think we don't, and the groups we belong to have an important bearing on our behaviour and attitudes. Understanding this psychology can teach us not just about the lives of fans, but about the dynamics of social change on a global scale.

2

Think Group

I N THE LATE 1960S, a social psychologist named Henri Tajfel
conducted a series of experiments at the University of Bristol
that would dramatically change our understanding of how people
behave when they're part of a group. Tajfel wanted to know why
we are predisposed to see other groups as different from our
own, and why we are so quick to disfavour them. Group prejudice
has played a role in some of the most important events of human
history. It affects many of the decisions we make every day.
Psychologists had been trying for decades to make sense of these
biases. They'd had limited success.

Tajfel was drawn to social psychology – the study of how we
are influenced by others – by his experiences during and immediately after the Second World War. His family were Polish Jews,
and almost all of them, in fact almost everyone he had grown
up with, died during the Holocaust. Tajfel survived because he
was a student in Paris when the Nazis invaded Poland, though
he spent much of the war as a prisoner. Afterwards, he did what
he would later refer to as the most important work of his life:
helping to rehabilitate refugees. By the time he entered academia,

at Birkbeck College in London, he was fixated on the big issues of human behaviour, such as identity, conformity, oppression and prejudice. Along with other Jewish social psychologists, he was determined to address what he believed were the two most important questions of their time: how had the Holocaust happened, and what could be done to ensure it never happened again? He thought the answers lay with deep-set social differences in nationality, culture, race or creed. His experiments in the 1960s showed that it was a lot simpler than that.

To test his ideas, he invited sixty-four adolescent boys from a local school into his lab and divided them into two groups. The groups were determined by seemingly trivial criteria, such as whether a boy overestimated or underestimated the number of dots on a screen, or whether he preferred paintings by Wassily Kandinsky or Paul Klee, artists none of them had heard of.[1] He then sent each boy to a cubicle, gave him a sum of money and a scorecard and asked him to distribute the money among the other pupils. Although the boys all knew each other, for the purposes of the study they were anonymous, identified only by a number and the group to which they belonged (more dots or fewer dots, Kandinsky or Klee).

Tajfel planned to gradually strengthen the criteria that defined his groups until he discovered the point at which the boys started to discriminate between their own group and others – or as he put it, the point at which group differences became meaningful. To his great surprise, this happened during the very first experiment. In a large majority of cases, boys who believed they had overcounted the dots on the screen gave more money to their fellow overestimators than to underestimators, and vice versa. Those who favoured Kandinsky over Klee were more generous towards other Kandinsky fans. The boys were consistently biased towards their own group, even though the boundaries between the groups were so flimsy that they barely existed at all. 'Outgroup discrimination is extraordinarily easy to trigger off,' concluded Tajfel.[2]

Let's think about this for a moment. The boys' decisions were not driven by self-interest: they had nothing to gain personally by penalizing those who didn't share their tendencies or tastes, and they did not know the identities of those they were giving to. Unlike previous studies of social prejudice, there was no backdrop of hostility, competition or conflict of interest between the groups (Tajfel called them 'minimal groups').[3] And yet the result was beyond doubt. The studies have been replicated many times: Tajfel himself obtained the same outcome after telling participants that the groups were determined by the random toss of a coin,[4] a state of affairs he considered 'the height of absurdity'.[5]

———

The minimal group experiments showed that people require little prompting to categorize themselves with others and to favour members of their own group over anyone else. Groupishness – the dance of 'us' and 'them' – is a certainty of social life. We categorize people all the time, on lines of race, gender, class, religion, nationality, profession and so on, to help us understand our social environment. This might be a reflection of our ancient past, when survival depended on cooperation and the ability to distinguish friend from foe. We evolved to live in groups, a reality that shapes almost everything we do.

Consider the groups you belong to: your family, friends,

neighbours, work colleagues, your children's school, a sports team, the local choir, the church, a fandom, perhaps a book club or a knitting class. I'm guessing they feel like a big part of who you are. Hopefully they give you companionship, purpose and a sense of security, and allow you to do things you wouldn't do on your own. Imagine who you'd be without them, what your life would look like. How would you survive?

After completing the minimal group studies, Tajfel, along with his colleague John Turner, spent the next few years developing a theoretical framework to explain why people spontaneously align themselves with others and how that affects their behaviour.[6] They believed that group membership gives people a distinct identity – they called it a 'social identity' – and that this provides 'some kind of meaning to an otherwise empty situation'.[7] A social identity gives us a sense of ourselves in relation to others: we are who we are because of what we share with our in-group and what we don't share with those outside it. Social identity is separate from personal identity, which reflects individual traits such as physical appearance and personality. During those moments when you feel an integral part of a group – watching a football match, for example, or attending a *Star Trek* convention – your social identity ('We're Trekkies!') will be more prominent than your personal one.

The groups we belong to have a big influence on our behaviour. We rapidly adopt their norms and needs, their ways of thinking and doing. They become a part of us just as we become a part of them. Group membership is transient: we can have many social identities, only one of which is likely to be active at any one time. If you work as a nurse, you may wear a uniform and fill your conversation with medical terminology while you're at the hospital, but you're unlikely to do that when you're with your college friends (unless they're also nurses). Most of us find slipping between our various social worlds as easy as putting on a new coat. Each world demands something different of us: a different identity, a different self. If you've ever made a friend in one environment (at work, say) and then observed them in another (with their family), you'll know how surprising and even disconcerting it can be to watch someone skip across their group boundaries.[8]

One of the most noticeable things about group behaviour is our propensity to act very differently towards people who are part of our in-group. We are friendlier towards them, more empathic, more generous, more attentive, quicker to help. We trust them more in all kinds of ways, which may explain why, during the pandemic, people believed that they were less likely to catch Covid from friends than from strangers.[9] We also feel their pain, quite literally.[10] This is not because we know or like them better (though that may be the case). It happens even with random groups, such as those in Tajfel's minimal experiments. It happens without us thinking about it. Brain imaging studies show that we generate more neural activity in the emotional centres of our brain when we interact with 'insiders' than when we interact with 'outsiders'.[11] In-group favouritism appears to be our natural default.

Tajfel and Turner's work led to a surge of interest in social behaviour, but they weren't the first academics to consider the ways in which groups distort the attitudes of their members. One of the most powerful descriptions of this universal human tendency is by the American social scientist William Graham Sumner in his book *Folkways*, published in 1906. Sumner coined

17

the word 'folkways' to refer to a group's social customs or ways of living. Most people, he observed, are set on their own road:

> Each group nourishes its own pride and vanity, boasts itself superior, exalts its own divinities, and looks with contempt on outsiders. Each group thinks its own folkways the only right ones, and if it observes that other groups have other folkways, these excite its scorn.[12]

———

Group identities can be as changeable as the weather. The decision to value someone or resent them, applaud or abuse them, notice or ignore them, can depend entirely on the context in which you meet them, or even what you are thinking about at the time.

In 2005, the psychologist Mark Levine and his colleagues at Lancaster University demonstrated this in an experiment involving football fans. Levine wanted to know whether someone would be more willing to help a stranger in distress if they knew they supported the same team. He recruited forty-five Manchester United fans, and following an introductory briefing at his lab sent each of them on a walk across campus. En route, Levine arranged for a jogger to run down a grassy bank and fall over in front of them, apparently injured. The jogger wore either a Manchester United shirt, a shirt of their bitter rivals Liverpool or a plain unbranded shirt. The researchers were interested in whether the choice of shirt would affect the participants' response. It did: they were three times as likely to come to the jogger's aid when he was wearing the colours of their own team.[13]

Levine then added a twist. He recruited another set of

Manchester United supporters, and this time at the introductory briefing he encouraged them to think of themselves not as Manchester United fans but as football fans in general – to dwell on their love for the sport rather than their love for their club. Under these conditions, primed with a different social identity, they proved equally willing to help the jogger whether he sported a Liverpool or a Manchester United shirt. The briefing had expanded their in-group so that it included all football-lovers. But not all humans: when the jogger wore the unbranded shirt, hardly anyone helped him. Group boundaries always have limits. It's where you draw them that counts.[14]

———

When people form a group, two things happen. The first is that the group feels compelled to distinguish itself from others – to signal its uniqueness. Its members may do this by wearing idiosyncratic colours (in a sports team), adopting an arcane ritual (in a faith group) or advocating a particular worldview (in a political party). The second thing is the pursuit of status: everyone wants their group to be as successful or prestigious as possible and tries to make it so.

This desire for distinction and status can have unfortunate consequences for outsiders. One of the easiest ways for a group to reinforce its credentials is to knock others down. Henri Tajfel's minimal group experiments showed us that bias can begin the moment a group's boundaries are defined. The history of the world has shown us that discrimination, prejudice, hatred and conflict follow close behind. Tajfel and other Jewish psychologists who had witnessed the Holocaust wanted to understand what caused this cycle. They feared that it would continue for ever. 'I share memories of a raging storm which – it seemed at the time – would never stop,' Tajfel wrote in 1981. 'Today, nearly forty years later, we have seen many new massacres and also some new holocausts.'[15]

But group behaviour is not destined to end in tragedy; the need for distinction does not always result in prejudice. For all his concerns about the potential of groups to cause conflict, Tajfel recognized that they are often a force for good, and that being part of one can be transformative. Stephen Reicher, a professor of psychology at the University of St Andrews, says Tajfel's theory of social identity has to do with differentiation rather than discrimination. 'We seek to make ourselves distinctive because the group is a source of meaning, of understanding. It's a way of positioning ourselves in the world. But you can differentiate yourself by being kinder to others, by being more generous, or whatever. You don't have to do it by being stronger, by doing the other down.'

Reicher is well placed to comment on Tajfel's work: he was an undergraduate at the University of Bristol when Tajfel was chair of the department. He remembers him being 'incredibly optimistic' about what people could achieve in groups. 'It's easy to see the group as the source of all problems, and that's where Henri started,' says Reicher. 'But he shifted round to seeing the group as a source of solutions. He saw that the group gives you social power. For me, to use a loose metaphor, groups are like dynamite: they can be used to construct, they can be used to destroy. The important thing is neither to be too pessimistic nor too Pollyanna-ish about them.'

Sometimes it is all too easy to be pessimistic. While writing this chapter, I watched along with the rest of the world as hundreds of disaffected Donald Trump supporters overran Capitol Hill in Washington DC, the seat of the US government, sparking one of the most serious constitutional crises in the country's history. Trump was the symbol of that group's identity, a relationship he habitually exploited during his presidency. In need of a scapegoat, he would simply conjure up an out-group for his supporters to denigrate: Mexicans ('drug dealers and rapists'), the Black Lives Matter movement ('a symbol of hate'), China ('the China virus'). Group psychology is this easily abused.

For the most part, this book errs on the side of Pollyanna. If Trump's shock troops reside in the dingy catacombs of group-land, most fandoms are in the sunny uplands. They teach us that being part of a group can give us a sense of belonging, do wonders for our mental health and help us achieve things we never could on our own. They also support the idea that group dynamics don't have to lead to intolerance. You can have in-group love without out-group hate, cooperation without conflict, winners without losers. Human social life is not a zero-sum game.

The psychologist Marilynn Brewer, a leading authority on rela-tions between groups, has spent much of her career championing this more upbeat assessment of collective behaviour. In the late 1960s and 1970s, she worked on a large study of inter-group customs and attitudes among thirty ethnic communities in East Africa. All the groups she looked at shared a tendency to divide their social world into in-groups and out-groups, and to rate the members of their own group higher than others on traits such as trustworthiness and honesty. But this bias did not result in intolerance; the two seemed completely unconnected.[16] 'These findings convinced me that in-group loyalty and favouritism are independent of outgroup competition or hostility,' she wrote in an email from her home in

Santa Barbara. She recalled a comment by one of her participants that seemed to echo William Graham Sumner's *Folkways*: 'We have our ways and they have their ways.'[17] Brewer believes that people form groups largely because they want to be with people of their own kind, and that human evolution owes more to cooperation within groups than competition between them.[18]

Brewer was gathering data from her field studies at the same time as Tajfel was working on his theory of minimal groups. In 1980, she visited him for three months at the University of Bristol and sat in on lab meetings as his team discussed their ideas about social identity. She came away convinced that, despite having different views about the inevitability of prejudice, both of them had landed on the same essential truth: that group identity is a basic feature of human psychology, and that as a constraint on human selfishness, it is what makes group existence possible.[19]

———

Even Brewer, champion of in-group love, is prepared to concede that certain circumstances, such as an environment of deliberate hostility, make out-group hate inevitable.[20] When states favour certain communities over others (as in Apartheid South Africa, Northern Ireland during the Troubles and the Palestinian Territories under Israeli occupation), different groups compete for a restricted resource (Sudan and the Democratic Republic of the Congo today), or political leaders manipulate ethnic or ideological divisions (Hitler in the 1930s), in-group loyalty grows ever stronger, and the out-group becomes an enemy.

We can add another example to that list: sport. It is hard to imagine conditions more conducive to non-lethal conflict. Sport is competitive by definition, which immediately raises the tempera-ture. Unlike most group activities, it *is* a zero-sum game: if I win, you lose. The results are unambiguous – there's no room for compromise. The predictable consequences of this – unreason-able love for one's own team, unreasonable prejudice towards one's opponent – are partly what make it so all-consuming. Bill Shankly, manager of Liverpool Football Club between 1959 and 1974, had it about right when someone suggested to him that football was a matter of life and death. 'It's much more important than that,' he replied.[21]

The most avid sports fans don't think of themselves as supporters of their team. They're greater than that: they *are* their team. In the language of Tajfel and Turner, their group identity overrides their personal one to the extent that they feel a part of it as much as any of the players. In *Fever Pitch*, Nick Hornby's memoir of life as a fan of Arsenal Football Club, he describes his obsession as an 'organic connection'. 'One thing I know for sure about being a fan is this,' he writes. 'It is not a vicarious pleasure, despite all appearances to the contrary, and those who say that they would rather do than watch are missing the point. Football is a context where watching *becomes* doing.'[22]

You can tell fans who identify strongly with their team by the way they speak. They might say, 'We won' or 'We lost', never 'They won' or 'They lost'. In social science, this use of the first person pronoun is known as the 'categorized we'. It allows the speaker to extend the boundaries of the self, to create a special category of inclusiveness. The only time the categorized we is heard outside of sports fandoms is when it is used to express national identity, as in 'We won the war' – which tells you a lot about a sports fan's level of engagement.[23]

The intensity is conspicuous not just in fans' language and behaviour, but in their biochemistry. During the 2014 World Cup in Brazil, Martha Newson, a cognitive anthropologist at the University of Oxford, ran a study to test cortisol levels in Brazilian football supporters as they watched their national team play. Cortisol is a hormone produced by the adrenal glands that helps us cope with stress; in situations where your social status is threatened, such as when your team is battling for survival, you'd expect your cortisol levels to max out.

Newson and her team organized public screenings of three of Brazil's games in the north-eastern city of Natal, taking saliva samples from fans as they watched. They found that their cortisol levels fluctuated during all three games, including two that Brazil won – hardly surprising, as watching your team play is always stressful. But they went through the roof when Germany beat Brazil 7–1 in the semi-final. It was Brazil's worst defeat since 1920. So many Brazilian fans left the screening at half-time, when their team was already losing 5–1, or were too distraught to cooperate by the final score that the researchers struggled to collect enough saliva samples for their study.[24]

The focus of Newson's research is on how group bonding affects behaviour. One of the aims of her World Cup study was to find out whether a fan's hormonal activity is linked to their level of commitment to their team. She has found in previous work with football 'ultras', military veterans and Libyan revolutionaries that people whose lives are defined by their membership of a group – whose personal and social identities have become highly aligned or 'fused' – show extraordinary levels of group loyalty, beyond even what they would show towards their own families. They are prepared to stick with their colleagues through good times and bad, and many of them are prepared to die for them. Desertion is unthinkable. 'For a strongly fused person, to renounce one's group membership would be tantamount to total rejection of one's present and past self, an epistemic and practical nightmare,' explains Newson in one of her papers.[25] Which suggests there is truth to the old cliché that while you can change your job, spouse, politics or religion, you can never change your football team.

Newson predicted that die-hard Brazilian fans, whom she identified through a survey before the game, would be more affected by the defeat to Germany than regular fans. This tends to be the penalty for high engagement: more pride and joy after a win, more sadness and anger after a loss. And so it proved: their cortisol levels were highest of all. Being a superfan is stressful when things aren't going your way.

———

If you're a sports fan, what sacrifices would you be prepared to make if they guaranteed your team a title victory? Daniel Wann, the leading psychologist specializing in sports fandoms, put this question to several hundred American baseball fans in 2011 to get an idea of their level of commitment. Of all those he asked, more than half said they would happily give up sex, shaving, sweets and all drinks except water for at least a month in order to secure the World Series title. A third claimed that they would forgo television. A fifth were willing to wear the same underwear or to stop talking to their best friend. A small minority were prepared to stop talking completely.

When Wann asked the fans what behaviours they might 'at least minimally consider', around half said they would contemplate donating an organ if it would help their team win the championship. That's commitment – or, if you're not a sports fan, idiocy. A bewildering 10 per cent of Wann's respondents said they might be persuaded to cut off one of their fingers, but I think we can assume that they misread the question. As you might expect, the would-be organ donors classed themselves as highly engaged fans, or as Martha Newson would say, 'fused'. 'Because they care so deeply about their team,' says Wann, 'and because being a fan is so central to their self-concept, they are willing to do almost anything for the team's success.'[26]

Sports fans parade their allegiances in weird and wonderful ways. One Arsenal fan named his daughter Lanesra, the name of his team spelled backwards. With any luck she grew up to be a Chelsea supporter. This is not inconceivable: such expressions of fan disloyalty regularly occur in families. Wann, a passionate fan of the Chicago Cubs baseball team, grew up in a family of St Louis Cardinals fans; his sole purpose in choosing the Cubs was to stand out from his father and irritate his older brother.

Most of us are happy to express our support by cheering loudly and engaging in what psychologists call BIRGing, or 'basking in reflected glory'. To BIRG is to make a show of your association with a successful team, despite having played no role in its achievement. The term was coined in the 1970s by the psychologist Robert Cialdini, who noticed that the number of students wearing clothing bearing their university's name or logo on US campuses increased after the college football team had won. A win always makes supporters feel good, and the students wanted in on the action.[27] Inevitably, they were far less keen to fly their team's flag after a defeat, preferring to hide their allegiance. Psychologists have an acronym for that, too – they call it CORFing, or 'cutting off reflected failure'.[28]

At first glance, BIRGing and CORFing seem like behavioural traits you might expect of fair-weather fans. Yet they stem from a psychological imperative we all possess: to maintain a positive sense of our own self-worth. We all want to feel good about ourselves. Being part of a group – sharing a history, a purpose, an identity – gives you that. When your team wins, you win. The more invested you are, the bigger the emotional pay-off. As we've seen, that cuts both ways: when a team loses, die-hard fans suffer the most. In *Fever Pitch*, Hornby confesses that his misery at Arsenal's misfortunes could reach 'monstrous, terrifying proportions'.[29] Die-hard fans never abandon their club, so how do they restore their shattered self-esteem? They take the only option available to them: dig in, reaffirm their loyalty, draw ever closer to their group, sling obscenities at opposing fans and remind each other that suffering breeds resilience. In a survey of clubs in the English Premier League between 2003 and 2013, Newson found that fans of Hull, the least successful team, reported the greatest number of social ties, a measure of close psychological kinship (fans of Chelsea, one of the most successful teams, reported the fewest).[30] Winning is important, but belonging is everything.

———

In 2015, I travelled to the Turkish city of Van, in the tectonically lively East Anatolian Highlands near the border with Iran. Four years earlier, in October 2011, a series of earthquakes had flattened thousands of buildings in the city, killing around 650 people and leaving tens of thousands homeless. I was writing a story about psychological resilience, and had come to Van to find out how the survivors were coping.

Earthquakes cause greater psychological trauma than any other natural disaster. The realization that the earth can swallow you up without warning can lead to a vast insecurity. It can be difficult for survivors to find their feet again, and to trust that life will continue. Immediately after the disaster, Turkish researchers estimated that nearly a quarter of Van's population had post-traumatic stress disorder, a prevalence in line with comparable events such as the 9/11 terrorist attacks on New York City and the 2010 Haiti earthquake. But the sociologists and psychologists I spoke to in 2015 were full of stories of recovery and hope. People had bounced back and found ways to live without fear. Most of the survivors considered themselves 'highly resilient', according to one survey.[31] Even those who had lost a relative or their home or had been injured themselves were doing better than many doctors expected.

What caused people to rally in such surprising ways? It was something quite mundane: social connection. On my second day there, I met Suvat Parin, head of sociology at the city's Yuzuncu Yil University, a neatly dressed, undemonstrative man who had lived in Van all his life and had become an authority on its social structure. Its social structure is how it survives, he said. 'Here in south-east Turkey, social bonds are everything. The social reality is a collective identity.' He described what happened to his own family immediately after the earthquake. He phoned his relatives to ask where they were and whether they were hurt, and they all arranged to meet, and within two hours they had gathered in the same place, a hundred survivors with the same surname.

They found some open ground and set up tents. They had everything they needed: food, medicine, clothing. 'It was all addressed in a collective manner. It gave us psychological leverage, a means to cope with things. Because you knew you were not alone, that there were people behind you.'[32]

Being part of a close-knit group has helped people live through situations even more extreme than the aftermath of an earthquake. Among Jews who were imprisoned in Auschwitz, those who arrived there with fellow prisoners from a previous camp were at least 20 per cent less likely to die. Having a social network gave them an advantage: moral encouragement, an identity, a chance of extra rations.[33] For the same reason, members of the Union Army who were imprisoned in the notoriously squalid and dangerous Confederate camps during the American Civil War were more likely to survive if they were held with friends from the same unit. Friendship protected them from a multitude of evils, and the degree of friendship mattered as much as the extent: the closer the bonds, the higher their chances of living.[34]

In the modern era, studies of political and military prisoners suggest that torture victims who belong to political organizations experience fewer psychological problems as a result of their ordeal than those with no political affiliation,[35] and that military personnel fare better in captivity than civilians. In both cases, social ties appear to play a crucial protective role. Nothing is more reassuring when you're up against it than to know that your buddies are rooting for you. Social support has also been found to contribute to the well-being of bomb-disposal officers, heart-surgery patients and many others under severe duress.[36] By the same token, the lack of it can make us extremely vulnerable. After the suicide bombings on London's transport network on 7 July 2005, survivors who weren't able to get through to their loved ones because the phone networks were down were at much higher risk of suffering substantial stress. In the wake of a disaster, simply talking to someone you know can make a big difference to how you cope.[37]

Psychologists refer to the healing effect of groups as the 'social cure'.[38] It can be remarkably powerful. A review of 148 health studies involving more than 300,000 participants in total found that social connection is more important to a person's health than commonly recognized factors such as smoking, exercise and diet.[39] It's a salve for the mind as well as for the body: people who have suffered depression are less likely to relapse if they join a group – and the more groups they join, the lower the risk.[40] The *quality* of connection matters. For a group to have healing powers – to offer protection from stress, increase resilience, speed up recovery or meet certain psychological needs – it has to feel emotionally significant.[41] Part of the reason for this is that people who regard each other as members of the same club – who share a social identity – are much more likely to help each other out. But feeling that we belong bestows its own psychological gifts: companionship, increased self-esteem, a sense of purpose, a feeling of control, a moral compass. It allows us to extend our loci of concern beyond our own well-being, to reach for a grander narrative for our lives and to find something meaningful in the things we share with others.

1. How important is it to you that the team wins?	1 = Not important 8 = Very important
2. How strongly do you see yourself as a fan of the team?	1 = Not at all a fan 8 = Very much a fan
3. How strongly do your friends see you as a fan of the team?	1 = Not at all a fan 8 = Very much a fan
4. During the season, how closely do you follow the team via any of the following: (1) in person or on television, (2) on the radio and (3) televised news or newspaper?	1 = Never 8 = Almost every day
5. How important is being a fan of the team to you?	1 = Not important 8 = Very important
6. How much do you dislike the team's greatest rivals?	1 = Do not dislike 8 = Dislike very much
7. How often do you display the team's name or insignia at your place of work, where you live or on your clothing?	1 = Never 8 = Always

Daniel Wann's Sport Spectator Identification Scale, an assessment of sports fans' commitment to their team. (International Journal of Sport Psychology)

———

The social cure applies to fandoms in the same way it applies to victims of trauma. For the past thirty years, Daniel Wann, the psychologist, has been interested in the connection that sports fans have with their team and their fellow fans and how this affects their well-being. His many studies have shown that fans who see their team as a central part of their identity – as an *extension* of themselves – have high levels of mental energy, self-esteem and happiness, and are also at lower risk of depression.[42]

What goes for sports fandoms applies to all fan groups. Since Wann started publishing his findings, other researchers have found a psychological dividend among fans of science-fiction films, fantasy books, boy bands, television dramas and Japanese animation films and comic books; or more specifically, among Trekkies (fans of *Star Trek*), Potterheads (*Harry Potter*), Sherlockians (Sherlock Holmes), Directioners (One Direction), Whovians (*Dr Who*) and *Star Wars* fans, who oddly haven't been afforded a common name that has stuck. Although many fans know each other exclusively through their online interactions, this doesn't seem to diminish the strength of their bonds. Researchers at the Queensland University of Technology interviewed several hundred science-fiction fans at a convention in Melbourne and discovered that they felt a greater sense of community with their fandom than with their neighbours.[43] Sharing a passion makes it so easy to connect.

Fandoms offer other benefits that are hard to quantify in scientific studies. The fantastical worlds of franchises like *Star Trek* and *Harry Potter* provide a refuge from the shortcomings of real life and a glimpse of how things could be different (more friendships, more magic). Being a fan allows you to be radical in original ways. Depeche Mode enjoyed a huge following in Eastern Europe during the Soviet era among people who wanted an alternative means to channel their frustration with the status quo. 'We are Depeche-ist, like Communist, or Fascist,' declares one fan in *The Posters Came from the Walls*, a documentary about the band's global following.[44] To this day, Russian fans celebrate 'Dave Day' on lead singer Dave Gahan's birthday, which also happens to be a national holiday, giving them a perfect excuse to parade their Depeche-ist sympathies.

Fandoms are places to breathe when the mainstream feels suffocating. It's safe to be different, weird or nerdy with your fellow fans, since you're all in it together. Thirty-five years ago, in a famous essay on fan culture, the media studies scholar Henry

Jenkins defined fandom as 'a vehicle for marginalised subcultural groups (women, the young, gays etc) to pry open space for their cultural concerns'.[45] Groups like these can become powerful forces for social change. In 2015, Rainbow Direction, a collective of LGBTQ fans of the boy band One Direction who had come together to fight homophobic bullying, achieved maximum recognition when members of the band started wearing their rainbow bracelets on stage.[46] Social interaction is the psychological fuel for this kind of activism.

One of my favourite examples of someone finding a home in fandom is Priyanka Bose, an Indian American writer living in Chicago who had always struggled to make friends until she became hooked on *Miraculous: Tales of Ladybug and Cat Noir*. *Miraculous* is a French television series about two teenagers with superhero alter egos who team up to protect Paris from a powerful villain. Priyanka joined an online *Miraculous* fan group and became friends, via the group chat, with three young women who also loved the show. Eventually she met up with them, and then she met their parents, siblings, spouses and even their pets. 'It feels unreal, in a world filled with so much unkindness, that a French children's show led me to such an incredible group of friends,' she wrote in the online magazine *Catapult* in December 2020. 'Together, we have created an oasis of love and friendship, where it's okay to be vulnerable, and where we deeply support each other's dreams and ambitions. It's miraculous, really.'[47]

That's the thing about fandoms: they can make people feel as if they're part of something marvellous. In the next chapter, we'll consider how people fall for their heroes in the first place, why they hold on so tightly to those fictive relationships, and the power that comes from sharing their passions with others.

3

Fictional Friends

BELIEVING A FICTIONAL CHARACTER to be real is a familiar cliché in popular culture. Without it, much drama would appear ridiculous. Some audiences are more susceptible to this than others. Take Sherlock Holmes fans. A good number of them are convinced that Arthur Conan Doyle's fictional detective is a real-life person. Many have written to him at 221b Baker Street, Holmes's address in Conan Doyle's stories. For more than half a century, their letters ended up at the Abbey Road Building Society (later the Abbey National), whose head office on Baker Street included number 221.

Until it vacated the premises in 2005, Abbey National employed a secretary whose sole responsibility was to answer these letters. Some of them included requests for intimate details about Holmes's private life. Was he left- or right-handed? Did he like gooseberry jam? Was he married? Had he ever made love to any of his clients? Various correspondents sought his opinion on vampires, poltergeists and other supernatural creatures. Others were more philosophical: 'How much is love the root of crimes?' Or plain eccentric: 'I have been collecting drawings of pigs by famous characters for some time and have recently been advised that you might be willing to furnish me with a pig drawn by your good self.' A large proportion requested Holmes's help in solving real-world crimes: the disappearance of a sister, the murder of an aunt, the theft of a Rolls-Royce. The identity of Jack the Ripper.[1]

These days, letters to Sherlock Holmes are delivered to the Sherlock Holmes Museum, which was awarded the 221b Baker Street address by Westminster City Council in 2010, despite being situated between numbers 237 and 241. Although Holmes has been 'retired' since 1904, there has been no let-up in fan mail. The museum receives five or six letters a day. A disproportionate number are from China, such as the following:

> Dear Mr Holmes,
> I'm writing to tell you bad news: Professor James Moriarty [Holmes's arch-enemy] is BACK! Last Friday, I saw him in a supermarket near my house, which is situated in Beijing, phoning somebody in a very low, but strange voice . . . I think it is an emergency and I'm looking forward to your early reply and your opinion.[2]

On a recent visit to the museum, an official told me that a correspondent from China had lately requested Holmes's help in securing him the affections of a woman who had refused his advances. Wherever they are, fans of Sherlock Holmes seem to be in no doubt that their favourite detective will assist them with any problem they might encounter.

———

Psychologists refer to this illusion of intimacy as a 'parasocial relationship'. You can have one with just about anyone, fictional or real, human or not. It's entirely one-sided, a relationship without reciprocity. You'll get nothing back. Equally, you'll never be rejected.

The concept might sound weird, but Donald Horton and Richard Wohl, the academics who coined the phrase in 1956,[3] believed that parasocial relationships were an expression of the fundamental human need to connect with others. They began their research at a time when mass media was in its infancy and popular fictional characters and celebrities with wide appeal were thin on the ground. Nowadays the choice is limitless, and parasocial bonds have become part of mainstream culture. If you're a fan of anything, you're in a parasocial relationship. Don't worry – it's perfectly normal.

As we saw in the previous chapter, building connections with others is an evolutionary imperative that drives much of our behaviour. Yet it can be hard to achieve: other people can be difficult, and relationships can make us vulnerable. It isn't very surprising that people sometimes prefer to invest their social energy in a fictional character and settle for a relationship over which they have greater control. Think of the advantages. Fictional characters are always available. They'll never ghost you. They have dependable personalities: you know what you're in for. And since a lot of other people are bound to like them too, they can bring a ready-made circle of human friends – like Priyanka Bose's *Miraculous* group, or the many friendships that have grown out of a mutual love for Harry Potter.

Psychologists do not advocate parasocial relationships as a substitute for the real thing, but there is plenty of evidence that they can benefit people.[4] First and foremost, they allow us to explore aspects of relationships that we may be anxious about, and to experiment with feelings of attachment and dependence without risk of harm. They offer the chance of growth: transporting ourselves to a fantastical world to interact with characters we will never meet in real life can be mind-expanding, not to mention a lot of fun. They also provide us with role models and attitudes to aspire to, as well as 'social snacks' – small reminders of what it's like to feel close to someone.

Occasionally, they can save a person's life. That's the way it seemed to twenty-seven-year-old Thea Gundesen, who as a young girl in Denmark during the early 2000s felt ostracized by her peers and desperately lonely. 'From an early age I did not fit in,' she told me. 'I was not like everyone else. I never felt accepted. They bullied me. They beat me. They ruined my things. Growing up knowing you don't belong is terrible. It may not seem like life or death but in a way it is.' Then her father brought home the video of *Harry Potter and the Philosopher's Stone*, the first film in the series, and she fell for its wondrous setting and joyful camaraderie. 'The wizarding world came as a bit of a saviour for me. I found solace there. Harry did not understand why weird things happened around him, why he wasn't accepted or loved. He was a wizard. He was different. And different was good. I realized that I wasn't weird, I wasn't alone, I just had not found my magical people yet who would understand me and accept me.'

Rather than identifying with a particular character in the franchise, Thea delighted in its alternative universe. She found it easy to teleport to Hogwarts and imagine herself taking part in adventures with Harry and his friends. 'It was a home far away from the life I was living, a whimsical place full of wonder and a community there to support you,' she says. 'It was the perfect fantasy. I felt no pain when I was there.' Since then, Thea has been diagnosed with Asperger's syndrome and attention deficit hyperactivity disorder (ADHD), which explains some of her childhood feelings of isolation and confusion. Today she cherishes her connection to the huge community of fans who share her love for Potterworld. Sometimes she conjures herself back there, keeping in mind the promise of wizard headmaster Albus Dumbledore that 'help will always be given at Hogwarts to those who ask for it' and his counsel to those who are struggling: 'Happiness can be found, even in the darkest of times, if one only remembers to turn on the light.'

Thea's experience shows that role models don't have to be real to be significant, and that the norms and values portrayed in fictional worlds can be just as relevant to our own.

Not long ago, I joined a conversation on the social networking platform Reddit in which fans of *Star Wars* discussed how the films had changed their lives. Many of them said they took inspiration from the Jedi, the ancient order of protectors who learned to channel the light side of the Force through meditation and the control of negative emotions. One fan said they aspired to be 'as level-headed, loyal, intelligent, witty and sarcastic' as Jedi master Obi-Wan Kenobi. Another, intrigued by the Jedis' mental discipline, went on to develop an interest in Buddhism. Several fans had managed to turn their childhood obsession with *Star Wars* into a philosophy for life. As one of them explained, 'The wisdom and ideals of the Jedi help me get through and remind me to be thoughtful about everything around me.'

Donald Horton thought that parasocial relationships would be of particular value to the perpetually lonely and socially anxious, giving them the 'chance to enjoy the elixir of sociability'.[5] Psychological research suggests this isn't necessarily the case: people who have difficulty relating to the feelings of other humans also have difficulty relating to imaginary characters, while extroverts and skilled communicators are proficient at both.[6] However, parasocial relationships *do* benefit people who have what psychologists call an 'anxious-ambivalent' attachment style: those who desire intimate relationships, but whose early life experiences have made them distrustful of them.[7] You can see why a fantasy figure might appeal to them: with no fear of abandonment, they are free to be as intimate and committed as they like. Another advantage is that if you know you can make a relationship work with Sherlock, Snape (from *Harry Potter*) or Spock (from *Star Trek*), you might be more inclined to take a chance with the friendly human who lives down the road.

Parasocial relationships are especially relevant when real-world relationships break down and we are left feeling desperate to belong. Social rejection can feel like a rupture at the core of our being. In the aftermath, people take great pains to rebuild ties with others or to create new ones, to darn the holes in their social fabric. They spend more time looking at family photographs, browsing their friends' profiles on social media or attending to symbolic objects such as a football shirt or a treasured gift, to reassure themselves that they are not alone.[8] They may even develop a closer relationship with their pet – anything to fill the void. In their urgency to connect, fictional characters are as likely to be recruited to the cause as living ones.[9] The psychologist Megan Knowles, who studies how people respond to rejection, says fictional characters can act as 'social surrogates' or substitute friends. Her experiments have shown that thinking about, writing about or watching a favourite character can alle-viate some of the harmful effects of rejection and act as a buffer against ostracism, just as real-life friendships do.[10]

People can be remarkably flexible when trying to meet their social needs. In her studies at the University of Houston, the psychologist Jaye Derrick has found that we can feel less lonely and less anxious in the face of rejection simply by *thinking* about a favourite television show.[11] One possible reason for this is that long-running shows such as *Grey's Anatomy*, *The Sopranos* and *Sex and the City* revolve around casts of characters who appear together in the same milieu week after week. It's easy to slip into that familiar space, and it gives us the experience of belonging. 'We get transported into this fictional social world,' Derrick explained. 'There is a plot, but there are also individuals, dyads and groups, and they are all interacting, and you get to feel like you are a part of that.' It's also likely, she says, that other people in our social networks are watching the same shows as us, perhaps even at the same time. 'These shows are social partly because we feel connected to our real close others when we watch them, or to online fan groups, or other large collectives that also care about them.'

Recently, a student of Derrick called Maggie Britton demon-strated that as well as changing the way we feel about ourselves, fictional worlds can help us change negative behaviours. Smokers wanting to quit, for example, are more likely to succeed if they have a supportive partner. Those with uncaring partners face a lonely struggle, but Britton has found that it's possible to compen-sate for a lack of support by turning to a favourite film, book or television show. Her research shows that a social surrogate is almost as effective as a human at helping them kick the habit.[12] Who needs a real-life partner when you can pour your heart out to Buffy the Vampire Slayer or the crew of the starship *Enterprise*?[13]

———

We spend a great deal of time in our fictional worlds. Why are we so fond of them? There are several possibilities. They offer an escape from our humdrum lives. They shield us from loneliness and social rejection. They help us see the world through the eyes of others and encourage us to imagine what they might be feeling. A popular theory among evolutionary psychologists is that fictional worlds allow us to simulate the future, try out new perspectives and prepare for scenarios that might threaten us.[14] All these could be true. For tens of thousands of years, humans have been dedicating a great deal of their cognitive energies to creating and consuming stories. It would be strange if they served no useful purpose.[15]

The appreciation of fiction is not a passive occupation. At its best it is deeply interactive, even transformative, a way of testing the boundary between imagination and reality. Its most visible manifestation is the art of cosplay, or 'costume playing', the fannish tradition of dressing up in a guise inspired by a fictional character.[16] Cosplay in its modern form originated at US science fiction conventions in the 1960s. It reaches its peak at San Diego Comic-Con International, the annual celebration of pop culture that attracts tens of thousands of fans each year. At Comic-Con, a visitor can expect to encounter at every turn elaborately styled imaginary beings such as Batman, Wolverine, Daenerys Targaryen, Lord Voldemort, a blue Na'vi from *Avatar* and any number of

Star Wars stormtroopers, Disney princesses, Princess Leias and Tolkien dwarves.

Henry Jenkins, the media studies scholar, describes Comic-Con as 'a field of dreams' and cosplay as a way of making those dreams public.[17] But the dreams are aspirational as well as fantastical. Cosplay allows fans to push the limits of what they can be and to experiment with their identities in playful ways. Cosplayers often deliberately pick characters that are very different from themselves, or characters of a different gender (known as *cross*play), or even of a different age, just to see what it feels like. Some choose characters with antisocial traits that they share but usually conceal – a chance to release their inner Darth Vader or Voldemort.[18]

Others embrace characters they would like to emulate, whose qualities or values they admire. In a study of 198 cosplayers recruited via social media, the psychologist Robin Rosenberg quotes a respondent who has wanted to cosplay as Wonder Woman for as long as she can remember:

Wonder Woman was a beautiful princess, but strong and independent. She took care of herself and everyone she cared about, and didn't need a prince to rescue her. Those were important qualities to me growing up in an all-woman household . . . In Wonder Woman I saw the best qualities of my mother, and the type of woman I wanted my sister and I to become. I've always idolized her from childhood and wanted to 'be' her when I grew up.[19]

To dress up as a personality from an imaginary universe and parade before a crowd of discerning fans requires a certain swagger. You might expect cosplayers to be extraverts or exhibitionists, yet personality surveys of this community have found the opposite.[20] They are dressing up not to show off, but because they love dressing up.

Once in character, their personalities can change significantly. The evidence for this comes mainly from studies of 'furries', fans of anthropomorphic animal characters (animals with human characteristics). Examples of anthropomorphic animals include Disney's Mickey Mouse and Bambi, the video game character Sonic the Hedgehog, the rabbits in Richard Adams's novel *Watership Down* and any of the animals in Rudyard Kipling's *The Jungle Book* or Disney's *The Lion King*.

Unlike other fans of popular culture, furries are not interested in existing characters; instead, they create their own. Every furry adopts a 'fursona', an avatar or spirit animal that represents an idealized or alternative version of themselves. A fursona can be any creature, real or mythic. The most popular are wolf, fox, dog (particularly husky), tiger and lion. The choice of species is influenced by culture: dragons are fashionable in Asia, and kangaroos in Australia. Some furries assume a hybrid identity: dog combined with wolf, for example. At furry conventions and in online forums, a vast array of less popular creatures jostle for space among the larger predators: rats, rabbits, raccoons, bears, horses, snakes, skunks, squirrels, ravens, owls and the occasional dinosaur. The research scientist Samuel Conway, organizer of the world's largest annual furry convention, Anthrocon in Pittsburgh, passes as a samurai cockroach. I have encountered griffins, unicorns and even a Quetzalcoatl, a feathered-serpent deity that was worshipped in ancient central America. Attending a convention allows furries both to express their inner animal and to feel part of a large, colourful family. If you fly the fur, you're part of the tribe. Accessories such as tails, ears, collars and fur-rimmed clothing are *de rigueur*, while the most committed don full-length fursuits that can take weeks to make. Whatever your look, a tail is regarded as a must-have: at furry conventions, it's always a good idea to check where you're putting your feet.

Furries may have a singular field of interest, but they share their motivation for expressing it with many other types of fans. 'It's an excuse to put like-minded people in the same room together,' says the social psychologist Courtney Plante. 'It's no different to the camaraderie and community in your local church group, or among football fans who go to the same pub every week.' Plante is co-founder of the International Anthropomorphic Research Project (IARP), a group of social scientists who have spent the last decade collecting data on the demographics, attitudes and behaviours of furries. Thanks to their research, we know more about furries than we do about any other fandom outside of sport.[21]

As a furry himself since he was a teenager, Plante knows his way around the fandom. His fursona is a neon-blue cat named Nuka – cat because they are his favourite animal, blue because, being colour-blind, it is one of the few colours he can see. He is comfortable sporting his furry credentials even in his role as a researcher. He sometimes lectures dressed in his fursuit (the feedback from students is 'largely positive', he says). When I reached him via Skype, at his office at Bishop's University in Quebec, Canada, he was wearing a leather collar attached to a chain-metal lead.

As well as being a furry, Plante is a 'brony' – a fan of the animated television show *My Little Pony: Friendship is Magic*. The series is based on the line of Hasbro toys that you may have played with if you grew up in the 1980s. Aimed at young girls, it has found an unlikely audience among twenty-something heterosexual men, who are drawn to its themes of friendship and compassion and enjoy the opportunity to overturn traditional gender stereotypes. The ponies in the show have idiosyncratic personalities as well as distinctive appearances: each of the six central characters ('the Mane Six') embodies an 'Element of Harmony' (Plante's favourite pony, Twilight Sparkle, stands for magic), and each episode ends with them learning a lesson about the nature of friendship.

Bronies, like furries, exhibit many of the behavioural tendencies predicted by Henri Tajfel and John Turner's social identity perspective that we explored in Chapter 2. Surveys carried out by Plante and his colleagues have shown not only that bronies identify with the positive social norms of the *My Little Pony* characters, but that those norms influence their behaviour. Bronies become more giving when they are in the company of other bronies: they donate more to charity and are generally more helpful. And the more they watch the programme, the more generous they become.[22]

The idea that qualities such as generosity are shaped by context jars with the idea that character is immutable, but this common perception appears to be wrong. Social psychologists generally accept that a person's social environment can have a profound effect on how they think and act, and even on their personalities. Social identity theory is founded on this principle,[23] and some of the evidence for it comes from IARP's research on furries.

In 2015, a team led by Stephen Reysen, a colleague of Plante, assessed several hundred furries for the 'Big Five' personality traits: extraversion, conscientiousness, openness to experience, agreeableness and emotional stability. They were tested twice: once in their everyday 'non-fan' identities and once 'in fursona'. The results were startling: in their fursona personalities, they scored significantly higher than in their everyday personalities on every trait, particularly extraversion. Changing their outer identity appeared to change their inner one. 'Fursonas tend to be bigger, larger-than-life versions of the self,' says Plante. 'So, happier and funnier, more outgoing and confident. But also more serious, more studious, friendlier. It's an idealised version.'[24]

This principle applies to other fandoms too. When Reysen assessed the personalities of sports enthusiasts in both fan and non-fan mode, he found a similar pattern, though the direction and magnitude of the changes were different. In team mode, sports fans were more extraverted but less conscientious, less agreeable and less emotionally stable. That sounds about right: on the terraces at a football match or in the bleachers at a baseball game, irascibility and confrontation are the norm. Being a fan may be transformative, but each fandom transforms us in its own unique way.

———

For all the joy and psychological growth that fictional worlds can bring, they sometimes leave us feeling frustrated. The plotlines may disappoint, the wrong characters fall for each other, or we may feel alienated when our particular age group, gender, ethnicity or sexual orientation is not represented. When this happens, fans often take matters into their own hands. The general rule in fandoms is, 'If you don't like it, rewrite it.' Millions of words of 'fan fiction' are written every day by people who want a different outcome, a different hero or a different lover for their hero. Almost none of it is shared beyond the fan communities that create it (E. L. James's *Fifty Shades of Grey* and Jean Rhys's *Wide Sargasso Sea* are notable exceptions).[25]

Modern fan fiction is commonly believed to have begun with *Star Trek*, whose fans have been boldly re-inventing their universe since the first series was broadcast in 1966. As a literary genre it goes back much further. Fans have been adapting stories and shaping narratives to their own ends since the birth of the modern novel. After the 1726 publication of Jonathan Swift's fantastical satire *Gulliver's Travels*, readers were so delighted by the hero's encounters with the miniature people of Lilliput, the giants of Brobdingnag, the flying island of Laputa and the Houyhnhnm talking horses that they made up their own adventures for him. *An Account of the State of Learning in the Empire of Lilliput*, for example, describes his encounter with a hubristic librarian who refuses to hand over any books unless Gulliver signs a declaration attesting to his 'vast erudition and learning'. The novel also inspired fan art, such as William Hogarth's engraving *The Punishment Inflicted on Lemuel Gulliver*, which depicts the Lilliputians performing an elaborate enema on Gulliver as punishment 'for his Urinal Profanation of the Royal Pallace at Mildendo'.[26]

Gulliver's Travels fan fiction was mostly homage to a much-loved creation. This is not always the case: dissatisfaction can be just as powerful an incentive. The least popular plot twist in nineteenth-century literature was Arthur Conan Doyle's decision to kill off Sherlock Holmes in 1893. In the years that followed, bereft fans resurrected Holmes hundreds of times in short stories and plays. Many of them were parodies that began by lampooning the great detective's name: *The Adventures of Chubb-Lock Homes*, or *Misadventures of Sheerluck Gnomes*, or a story about the endeavours of 'Thinlock Bones' and 'Dr Watsoname'. Eventually the author himself had a change of heart and brought Holmes back to life for *The Hound of the Baskervilles* in 1901. Doyle's canon of detective stories has since been spun off, re-imagined and adapted for television and radio more times than any other work in English.[27] The fan fiction catalogue continues to grow. A popular trope is '221b' – stories that are precisely 221 words long and whose last word ends in 'b', a salute to the hero's address on Baker Street.

Fan fiction is endlessly creative. Archive of Our Own, one of the largest online repositories of fan fiction, art and video, has around five million registered users and holds more than nine and a half million works (these numbers surged during the coronavirus pandemic).[28] On Archive of Our Own you can find extravagantly imagined stories about almost any character in popular culture, real or fictitious, along with reframed plotlines of thousands of television shows, films, novels, plays, comics and graphic novels. There are more than 10,000 versions of *The Hobbit*, and 400 of *War and Peace*. A common approach is to relocate the action in the twenty-first century . . .

After the duel, Pierre decides to take his frustrations to reddit.[29]

or to reframe it in ways that may appeal more to modern audiences. Tolstoy almost certainly never considered this alternative opening to his classic novel:

Natasha wonders, often, about the ethics of finding solace in her dead fiancé's sister.[30]

Fan fiction offers surprising and sometimes bizarre versions of both real and imaginary worlds. If you don't read fan fiction, you won't know that the members of One Direction have been reborn as Hollywood superstars, or that Batman and Ironman were class-mates at boarding school before they became superheroes, or that Fox Mulder from *The X-Files* met God, or that Captain Kirk, Dr Spock and Bones travelled to Earth to meet the actors who play them in *Star Trek*. The Regency adventures of the hammer-wielding superhero *Thor* and his involvement in a *Sense and Sensibility*-style double-marriage plot will have passed you clean by.

A major preoccupation of fan-fiction writers is the invention of relationships that don't appear in the original, a practice known as 'shipping'. Shipping two of your favourite characters is a way to develop or understand them, to explore what they are capable of. It is common in fan fiction to ship two same-sex characters who aren't necessarily gay, a trope that has become known as 'slash fiction' (after the punctuation symbol used to depict the pairings). Slash fiction allows fans to re-imagine traditional narra-tives and disrupt the social or sexual dynamics in their favourite works, a strategy that can be both empowering and liberating.

The original slash ship is Kirk/Spock, a *Star Trek* liaison that was apparently just waiting to happen. Other common couplings include Holmes/Watson, Starsky/Hutch, Bond/Q, Bodie/Doyle (from *The Professionals*) and Willow/Tara (from *Buffy the Vampire Slayer*). Not all slash pairings are quite so obvious. Students of ancient English history may be surprised to learn about Arthur/Merlin. My mother and her church friends would certainly raise an eyebrow at Jesus/Judas. A whole sub-genre known as 'popslash' focuses on imaginary liaisons between members of the nineties pop groups NSYNC and Backstreet Boys. 'Larry Stylinson' is the sobriquet for the longed-for and almost certainly fictional romantic relationship between Harry Styles and Louis Tomlinson of One Direction. The Japanese comic *Hetalia: Axis Powers*, whose characters are personifications of the nations that fought in the Second World War, has delivered us America/England, which represents a hook-up between an energetic young man with starry blue eyes and an irritable one with terrible cooking skills (no points for guessing which is which).

In recent years, slash-fiction writers have been consumed with the abundance of possibilities that exist in the Harry Potter series. The Potter fandom is the largest literary community on the web. It has registered more than 370,000 works on Archive of Our Own, twice as many as the next most prolific, *Star Wars*. Many Potterheads would be aghast at the idea of Harry/Hermione, Harry/Ron or Harry/Draco, but these and hundreds of other unforeseen unions are out there for all to read. J. K. Rowling's imaginary universe is already both sophisticated and diverse, so why the need to expand it? Fans will always think there is more of the story to be told. Rowling would not recognize many of the subplots and characterizations in Harry Potter fan fiction, but in the fandom the versions written by devotees are considered just as valid as the original.[31]

You may have noticed that slash fiction pairings are nearly all male. This could be related to the fact that most of the authors are women. (80 per cent of users of Archive of Our Own identified as female in its latest census, in 2013.)[32] Ever since the early days of *Star Trek*, most highly engaged pop culture fans have been women – relatively few Trekkies fit the popular stereotype of the maladjusted male who speaks Klingon and greets his friends with a Vulcan salute. The most likely explanation for this gender variance is that the majority of television shows are made by men and portray a masculine perspective; participating in a fandom and writing fan fiction has allowed women to create a narrative that reflects the society they would like to see.[33]

Lately, other disenfranchised and minority groups, such as people of colour, the LGBTQ community and those with disabilities, have followed suit, flocking to fan sites and reshaping their favourite stories and characters in ways that represent them better. Fan fiction is a broad church, and it is eating away at the patriarchy: white heterosexual men account for a tiny and ever-diminishing minority of authors.[34] In 2013, the fantasy writer Lev Grossman observed that fan fiction had become far more bio-diverse than the mainstream works it parodied:

> It breaks down walls between genders and genres and races and canons and bodies and species and past and future and conscious and unconscious and fiction and reality. Culturally speaking, this work used to be the job of the avant garde, but in many ways fanfiction has stepped in to take on that role.[35]

A decade on, fan fiction is more experimental and heterogeneous than ever, regularly tackling issues that rarely surface in the mainstream. It embraces apocalyptic futures, male pregnancy, accelerated and reverse ageing, the swapping of bodies and genders, time travel, incest, reincarnation and every sexual inversion and perversion you might care to imagine. Its categories cover centaurification (when a character shape-shifts into a centaur), 'aliens made me do it' (have sex, basically), 'mate or die' (as it sounds), 'wing fic' (humans grow wings), 'curtain fic' (in which heroes do domestic chores), 'death fic' (the death of characters that survived in the original), 'dark fic' (stories notably more depressing than the original) and, most pleasingly of all, 'coffee shop fic', in which the protagonists find romance over a cappuccino or a macchiato.

One of the fastest-growing categories of fan fiction is political fic. Much of it, like this example, seems to centre on the love life of Bill and Hillary Clinton:

> Bill spun her around and pulled her back into his arms. 'The right wingers over by the bar are watching every move we make.' 'Yes, I know.' She placed her hand on his chest and his hand immediately covered hers. 'I can practically hear the wheels turning in their heads from here.' 'Well, you know baby they don't use their brains that often so they're bound to be rusty and noisy.' (*The Same Old Thing* by RacingHeart)[36]

If that feels too realistic, you could try some of the improbable fare about Donald Trump's relationship with Shrek:

> Trump suddenly felt strong arms surrounding him, steadying him and saving him. He looked up at the man who held him, and found himself losing his breath once again as Shrek brought his large callused hands towards his head. 'Looks like your toupee slid a little,' Shrek breathed in his ear as he righted Donald's hair with a gentle touch that was unexpected of an ogre of his stature. (*Make America Green Again* by orphan_account)[37]

Or this spectacularly weird skit about David Cameron's first night in office, when he meets Hermione Granger, his self-appointed Secretary of State for Magical Affairs:

'Magic doesn't exist,' David tells her. 'Magic is fairy tales.' Granger sighs, snaps her fingers and suddenly his whole office is full of birds of paradise. They fly around the top of the room, squawk, shed a bit, and disappear. (*A Historic and Seismic Shift* by raven (singlecrow))[38]

People write fan fiction for all kinds of reasons. It allows them to participate more fully in a narrative they love, and even to subvert it; to get inside the minds of their favourite characters; to stay a little longer in a story they don't want to end; to explore their own identity through the eyes of others; to escape their own reality or try out a new one; or to test their writing skills on an audience that won't judge them. Writers of fan fiction often develop long-term parasocial relationships with the characters they write about, and may feel they know them better than the person who created them.[39] Along the way they gain human friends, for writing fan fiction is a social activity. If you're intent on taking Harry Potter to places that J. K. Rowling never did, it's important to know where other fans have already taken him, and to participate in that community of writers. You can be sure that you'll have at least two things in common: a love of writing and a love of whatever it is you're writing about.

In the early stages of my research for this book, I went to a 'fan studies' conference at the University of Portsmouth – a sort of convention for academics. Most of those attending were 'aca-fans' – researchers who had turned their childhood passion into a subject of scholarship – but the stand-out presentation was delivered not by an aca-fan but a writer and publisher of fan fiction.[40]

Atlin Merrick has written more than a million words of fan

fiction, more than 60 per cent of which is about Sherlock Holmes. Her Sherlock stories, which are hugely popular on Archive of Our Own, are re-imaginings of the ways in which the great detective and his associate John Watson could have met, as friends or romantic partners, other than at St Bartholomew's Hospital in London in 1881. So far she has written 110 versions of this motif. She has brought the pair together, across the decades, in a West End strip club, an empty house during the Blitz, a computer lab in Hong Kong, Wandsworth Gaol, a King's College lecture theatre, a police station in India, Waterloo Station (where they meet as lost children) and a pedestrian tunnel beneath Southwark Bridge. At their heart, she says, they are stories of friendship. 'If you don't have the friendship, you don't have Holmes and Watson.'[41]

In her presentation, Merrick talked about the friendships she has made as a member of fandoms and a writer of fan fiction, and how they have 'changed everything' for her. 'Fandoms give people power,' she said. Later, I asked her what she meant. She explained that in the wake of the Black Lives Matter movement, it had become clear that society is often blind towards people who are different. 'Can you imagine being an asexual autistic dyslexic person? You're so specialized and so small that you're invisible. If the entire black community is invisible, what chance do you have of being seen? But then you write a story and some-body reads it, or you read a story and you recognize yourself in it. You see that you are valid. That's the power.'

In today's culture, it often feels like the power lies elsewhere – with the stars or the corporate machines that drive them. Being a fan is a way of taking it back. The next chapter focuses on fans of celebrities, a category that attracts a disproportionate amount of media attention. Here more than anywhere, adoration crosses over into obsessiveness and occasionally delusion. Yet parasocial relationships with celebrities are mostly rewarding and sometimes life-changing. Stars need their fans – the history of popular culture would look very different without them.

4

Reach for the Stars

CELEBRITY-WORSHIP IS OFTEN THOUGHT of as an exclusively modern phenomenon, but it has a long history. Among the first people to venerate popular figures in their culture were the ancient Greeks. Their heroes were mythical warriors, most of whom became heroic by killing – or sometimes dying – in battle. Achilles, the protagonist of Homer's *Iliad*, made his name by slaughtering numerous Trojan warriors during the battle for Troy.[1] One of his victims was Hector, a hero in his own right, who Achilles dispatched while promising to hack away and eat his flesh (in Achilles' defence Hector had just killed his friend Patroclus, along with 31,000 Greek soldiers). Most valiant of all was Heracles, son of Zeus, celebrated for slaying the nine-headed hydra of Lerna, among other achievements.

These icons of ancient Greece were immortalized in statues, paintings, songs and legends, but they can hardly be held up as paragons of virtue. Heracles beat his music tutor to death with a lyre and also killed his own wife and children, albeit in a state of madness provoked by his hateful stepmother. Achilles was proud, bloodthirsty and vengeful: after killing Hector, he tied his body to a chariot and dragged it through the dust for twelve days. Despite their questionable behaviour, these men were cult heroes, the celebrities of their day.[2]

Classicists argue that the ancient Greeks revered their heroes because they were prepared to sacrifice themselves to help others, a motivation that modern celebrities generally lack. Still, as we shall see in this chapter, many of the qualities we value in celebrities are similar to those that the Greeks appreciated in Achilles, Hector and Heracles. Modern-day fans are drawn to their idols because of their accomplishments – we are impressed by skill and achievement and raise on a pedestal those who excel. Tastes change: these days we prefer excellence in music, literature, sport, drama and art to mass murder, though serial killers have their fair share of admirers. Once we've found our heroes, just like the ancient Greeks, we still look to them for redemption.

Why do we need them? One explanation comes from a series of experiments by the psychologist Albert Bandura. In the 1960s, Bandura suggested that people learn how to behave largely by observing and imitating others (this is known as social-learning theory). This may sound obvious today, but it was considered radical at a time when most psychologists believed that people learn by being rewarded or punished for their responses to changes in their environment (the so-called 'stimulus-response' model).

Bandura tested his theory by studying children as they interacted with a Bodo doll – a life-size inflatable figure with a bulbous base that bounces back up when you knock it over. Initially the children watched while an adult played with the doll. Sometimes they behaved aggressively towards it, punching it in the face or throwing it around the room; other times they ignored it completely. When the children took their turn, they tended to copy whatever the adult had done. Those who had observed the aggressive adult wasted no time in laying into the doll with fists, feet and verbal abuse, while the others paid it no attention and busied themselves with other toys that were lying around.[3]

The Bodo doll experiments demonstrated how children are influenced by those around them. They also revealed something about the importance of role models. The results showed a strong gender bias: boys were more likely to imitate men and girls to imitate women. In the real world, we are apt to emulate people who are like us. They might be similar in gender, race or age, or have had comparable experiences, or be closely aligned to us in values or personality.[4] An affinity on any of these parameters is a good predictor of whether we'll favour someone, identify with them or seek to emulate them. It's how we choose our friends – and our heroes.

———

Anyone studying the psychology of celebrity will sooner or later encounter the research of Gayle Stever. A professor at Empire State College in New York, she has been exploring the subject for more than three decades. Unusually among researchers in this field, she has never been a fan of any celebrity she has studied. She is, however, a fan of fans – what she calls a 'metafan'.

Stever's fascination with fandom began when she was nine years old in the mid-1960s. The Beatles had just released a new record, and she was queuing with her mother outside Sibley's department store in Rochester, New York, hoping to buy a copy. 'They opened the door – it was all adults, I was the only kid – and all of a sudden it was run or be trampled. I was running through the store with these crazy people around me and I'm like, what is going on here?'

Stever has pursued that question her whole career. She engages in 'participant–observer ethnography', a field-based approach to research that involves hanging out with fans in their natural habitats – concert venues, fan conventions, press conferences and award shows. She has attended dozens of concerts by stars such as Michael Jackson, Paul McCartney, Madonna, Janet Jackson, Josh Groban, Celine Dion and Michael Bublé, and more than a hundred *Star Trek* conventions. She remains an outsider looking in, whether she is standing in queues and interviewing fans, distributing questionnaires or making notes on what she observes. She is, however, meticulous in conducting her due diligence: she once watched five seasons of *Star Trek: The Next Generation* in a few weeks to bring herself up to speed and ensure the fans would take her seriously.[5]

It's easy to see why Stever is good at her work. She has a natural way of making conversation and wears her opinions lightly. You can imagine her winning the confidence of fans as they stand in line outside a concert venue or convention centre, steering the banter towards the subjects that interest her. She started out, in 1988, studying Michael Jackson fans, who she quickly discovered did not fit the stereotype favoured by the media, which presented them as needy, grasping and obsessive. 'I went to my first show with a mental image of what I thought those fans were going to be like and I had to throw it all out,' she told me. The first thing she noticed was that the vast majority of them were adults: Jackson was thirty at the time and most of his fans were within five years of his age. The second thing was how well adjusted they were.

Passionate adult fans are often assumed to be pathological or irrational (this doesn't seem to apply to sports fans). Stever says that the fans she met were 'normal people carrying on normal lives, with functioning relationships and jobs, who just had this passion for Michael Jackson or Josh Groban or *Star Trek*'. They were fanatical but not frenzied, obsessed but not obsessive. She says that in her thirty years of research and thousands of interviews, she has met 'maybe fifteen' fans who were unwell, including one who used extensive plastic surgery to make himself look like Michael Jackson. Most fans in Stever's studies view their relationship with their idol as similar to an important friendship or a special hobby. They perceive themselves to be *like* their hero: almost every male Michael Jackson fan she assessed believed they shared a personality type with Jackson (the introverted-intuitive-feeling type on the Myers–Briggs scale, which is not typical of men generally). 'They would say things like, "I don't feel I'm in step with the rest of the world, but I'm like Michael and I identify with him",' she recalls.[6] We are often drawn to people who we perceive to be like us, and this seems to be as true for parasocial relationships as real-life friendships.[7]

Level	Description
Level 1	Negative interest in the star. Is an "anti-fan."
Level 2	No interest in stars or in being a fan of anyone.
Level 3	Average interest in celebrities but without any clear interest in any individual or individuals.
Level 4	Above average interest in stars or media without the emphasis on one particular star. Obviously a media fan but not a specific fan of one individual.
Level 5	Interested in a star or small group of stars to the exclusion of others but interest is limited to the stars' work (not the stars as people).
Level 6	Interpersonal interest in star that exacts a considerable cost to the fan in time, money and effort to follow the star. In spite of this cost, interest is not obsessive and does not chronically interfere in daily life.
Level 7	Obsessive interest in the star to the point where the interest intrudes on the everyday reality of the fan. High functioning in everyday life in spite of the obsession (has a job, family, etc. and meets obligations in this area).
Level 8	Interest is clearly pathological in that it affects the fan's health in a negative way, prompts occasional (or chronic) suicidal ideation, or in some other way is clearly not in the best interests of the fan. Interferes with the pursuit of normal employment and/or family and significant relationships.

Gayle Stever's Fan Intensity Scale, which measures fans'
level of interest in celebrities. (Gayle Stever)

Parasocial relationships with celebrities can yield many benefits. In 1988, Stever went to see a seventeen-year-old girl whose father had recently left the family home. The girl was an avid Michael Jackson fan and her bedroom walls were covered with posters of her hero. She had been very close to her father. She told Stever, 'I love Michael Jackson and he won't leave me. If I decide I don't want to follow him anymore, I can take all this down and be done with it, but it will be my decision.' It was clear that Jackson was helping her process her grief at the loss of her relationship with her dad.

Twenty years later, Stever met a woman outside a Josh Groban concert whose husband had died of an aggressive form of cancer. The woman had discarded the notion that she might have another relationship because she didn't think she could feel for anyone the way she had felt for her husband. Then she developed a crush on Groban. She knew it was silly – he was far too young for her, and in any case she'd never get to meet him – but it made her realize that she was able to have romantic feelings. She even considered the possibility that she might date again. 'I've heard that story many times,' says Stever. 'I've met many women – they all happen to be women – who mitigated the pain of their loss by forming this connection with somebody who was safe and distant, who wasn't going to put any demands on them. It gives you the opportunity to test out your feelings on a safe object instead of a colleague or neighbour.'

Celebrity crushes are not always quite so affirmative. They can sometimes lead to unrealistic expectations, particularly for younger people who have little experience of real-world relationships. Riva Tukachinsky, a colleague of Stever, has found that adolescents who have intense emotional attachments to celebrities often develop idealized notions of what a normal relationship should be, believing, for example, that they should like everything about the person they are with, or that good relationships are free of conflict. No doubt real life quickly robs them of such illusions.[8]

———

For many fans, their idol becomes a role model, someone they seek to emulate. In 2020, I spoke with a British Indian woman in her thirties who has 'loved' Michael Jackson for as long as she can remember.[9] When she was a teenager, she filled her bedroom walls with pictures of the singer, but her devotion was not so much a romantic ideal as an acknowledgement of the values he stood for. 'His message was all about caring for the planet, caring for each other, doing good things. I appreciated that. It inspired me. I wanted to care about other people and be kind and compassionate. My parents instilled very similar values. They didn't drink or smoke. Michael Jackson didn't do drugs, so there was no way in hell I was touching that. He didn't smoke, and I wasn't going to do that. As far as I was aware, he didn't drink, so I didn't want to drink. To this day, I've never tried a cigarette or any kind of drug and I've never had a drink. A lot of that I can put down to Michael's influence.' She is, of course, fully aware that the abusive behaviour Michael Jackson has lately been accused of is at odds with these values, a dissonance I address in Chapter 7.

Sometimes we are drawn to a celebrity because they represent something – an attitude or a way of being – that previously seemed closed to us. The screenwriter Jane Goldman, whose credits include *X-Men: First Class*, *Kingsman: The Golden Circle* and *Kick-Ass*, was a fan of Boy George in her early teens, partly because she loved his music and partly because his androgynous appearance and uniquely flamboyant style made her believe she could achieve something in life other than what was expected of her. 'I saw in him this drive and this possibility of going out and living slightly outside of what society tells you to do,' she told me. 'He inspired me to say, I'm going to forge my own path.' Which she did, leaving school after completing her O-Levels and hustling a job as a journalist at the music magazine *Smash Hits*. This was a bold move for a fifteen-year-old in the 1980s, and Goldman suggests that it might not have happened without her idol's influence. 'I remember the first time I saw him on *Top of the Pops*, it was like something clicked. I've spoken to a lot of people who have had the same experience. I felt like an outsider, I wasn't quite sure where I fitted in the world, and then I suddenly had a sense of belonging, like I had found my way.'

These fans' assessments of their connection to their heroes correspond with some of the latest thinking in social psychology on the relationship between leaders and their followers. In the popular imagination, great leaders, role models and heroes are characterized by qualities of personality, such as strength, charisma and intelligence. But social psychologists have found that a leader's effectiveness depends on how well they reflect the values, norms and aspirations of their followers, rather than on their individual traits. Influential leaders are a symbol of their group's social identity; they are easy to follow because their values match those of their followers. By this reckoning, Donald Trump was popular in 2016 because despite his great wealth he managed to position himself as a hard-working, regular American; he was the politician who disliked politicians and thus appealed to those who had become disillusioned with the political elite. Taylor Swift's millions of young fans love her for her music but also for her awareness of the things that matter to them, such as the rights of women and the emotional turbulence of adolescence. They don't know her, but her songs make it clear that she knows them.[10]

We love our celebrity heroes because of what they stand for, or because we want to be like them, or because we think we are like them. Sometimes, we love them simply because they are exceptionally good at what they do. The millions of tennis fans who idolize Roger Federer, who belong to all ages, classes and nationalities, flocked to his matches with what seemed like religious devotion. In a famous essay published in the *New York Times* in 2006, the novelist David Foster Wallace argued that Federer is afforded this level of reverence because his genius cannot be explained by science. '[He] is one of those rare, preternatural athletes who appear to be exempt, at least in part, from certain physical laws . . . a type that one could call genius, or mutant, or avatar. He is never hurried or off-balance. The approaching ball hangs, for him, a split-second longer than it ought to . . . he looks like what he may well (I think) be: a creature whose body is both flesh and, somehow, light.'[11] It reads like a paean to a hero of ancient Greece – or a god.

———

Celebrity fan culture as we know it today emerged in the early twentieth century when cinema became the principal form of mass entertainment. In the 1930s, a quarter of a million fan letters arrived at Hollywood's film studios each month; a top star could expect to receive three thousand a week. Some of them were marriage proposals. Some contained gifts. Most of them were requests for photographs or personal souvenirs: a button from Clark Gable's dinner jacket; a wishbone from Fred Astaire's Christmas turkey, if you please.[12]

Fan letters – distinct from autograph requests – tend to come from the extreme fringe of a fandom. In the 1990s, Gayle Stever helped two actors from the television series *Star Trek: Deep Space Nine* deal with their correspondence. 'I went through all their fan mail for a period of three years and I can tell you it's not representative at all of who the fans are,' she said. 'I knew most of those involved in their fan club at that point, and I never encountered a letter from anybody I knew.'

Still, fan mail can be instructive, not least because it demonstrates the extent to which some fans become consumed by their heroes.

Dear David Bowie,
Please forgive me if I am disturbing you, but you are my central life. I wish I could be in your arms and forget who I am and feel protected and secure with your love. What a dream! What strange feelings!

Dear David,
Sometimes I am so afraid that something will happen to you that I can't breathe, I am so afraid. Please come to me soon!

Dear David,
You are my vision of man, the original beyond all the rules we've ingested to control our thoughts and actions.

These extracts are from letters collected by the cultural commentators Fred and Judy Vermorel in the 1980s as part of a project to record the social history of pop music fandom. Over four years, they read forty thousand fan letters, conducted three hundred and fifty hours of interviews and analysed four hundred diaries, questionnaires and dream journals.[13] David Bowie featured prominently; many of his fans seemed to view him as an emanation of the divine.

He came to us a bit like Jesus. You could also call him an alien. (Sheila)

I began to think he was a new kind of Messiah. (Julie)

At first I was into the music, then I got into the man. It became a religion, an all-consuming adulation. (Melanie)

Bowie was the subject of countless sexual fantasies among his fans. One woman regularly imagined making love to him at the top of a mountain. Another dreamed that he scratched off her breasts with his fingernails and ate them. In his power to arouse, Bowie was outclassed only by Barry Manilow, who was a particular favourite with married women.

Me and my husband only live together now as brother and sister . . . I just feel unclean with any other man apart from Barry. If I can't have sexual intercourse with Barry, I'll go without. (Rosie)

When I make love with my husband I imagine it's Barry Manilow. All the time. (Joanne)

Some of these fans felt shameful about their secret passion, believing it made them weird or morally corrupt. All of that disappeared when they joined their local fan club, where suddenly they found themselves with a set of friends who were as passionate and secretive as they were. 'I expected people to be walking in with paper bags over their heads and dark cloaks and collars pulled up, and all looking round with shifty eyes and sneaking in through side entrances,' recalled Helen, a committed 'Manilover', after her first fan club meeting. 'But they'd got pictures on the wall and people had T-shirts on and were flying their colours very proudly.' Her fellow fan Rosie (one of those quoted above) built her entire social world through the fan club after the death of her mother. 'Without Barry and all these dear friends I've made through him I don't know how I could have coped with life,' she said. 'I mean no one can take my mum's place, but he's certainly done a very good job trying to.'

At the end of their project on pop music fandoms, the Vermorels appeared to be conflicted about their findings. In the afterword of their published work, they point to an undercurrent of hostility in many of the fan letters and interviews, a consequence, perhaps, of all that 'unconsummated, unconsumable passion'. The way fans responded to the blatant provocations of their idols by subverting the power to their own ends seemed like a political act:

> The closer you look at fans the less they seem like devotees of any particular act than the priestesses/priests of a disturbing kind of consumer mysticism . . . In their passion, in their ecstasies, in their delirium, fans show themselves to be the true heirs of utopian Romanticism, a current of sensibility which has consistently proved itself more troublesome, more subversive and more challenging than many a professed radicalism.[14]

In the history of pop culture, no one has inspired passion, ecstasy and fantasy quite like Elvis Presley. Numerous women he had never met were convinced they were married to him. Several believed they had borne his children. A woman called Bess Carpenter, an Elvis fan since the age of fourteen, was confident he had been present at the birth of her son:

> The doctors and nurses were all around me in these white gowns, looking at me. Right there among them, Elvis Presley appeared. He smiled and winked at me. He said, 'Relax, Bess, it's OK. I'll

be here with you.' It looked just like him . . . Then, when the baby came, it was he who said, 'It's a boy!' For an Elvis Presley fan, there can't be a bigger thrill than hearing Elvis himself telling you you have a new baby.[15]

Remarkably, Elvis's power has hardly diminished since his death. There are still nearly four hundred active Elvis fan clubs around the world, with more than 1.7 million members between them.[16] He continues to draw the widest possible constituency: his fans are of all ages and from all cultures. One measure of his enduring appeal is the number of people who make a living impersonating him, estimated at fifty thousand worldwide.[17] 2022 saw the release of yet another biopic, Baz Luhrmann's Elvis. He has been dead for nearly fifty years, yet we cannot seem to let him go.

Despite multiple sightings, Elvis wasn't available for interview, so I opted for the next best thing: Ben Thompson, one of the most acclaimed Elvis tribute artists out there.[18] In 2018, he won the Ultimate Elvis Tribute Artist Contest in Memphis, which is rather like winning a Grammy. When you meet Ben, the idea that he could be Elvis seems improbable. He is from Croydon in south London, and was born nearly two decades after Elvis died. Off stage, he is unpretentious, extremely affable and without a hint of swagger. On stage, he is completely different, and a dead ringer for the King. He doesn't just resemble him, he *embodies* him. In his voice, moves, mannerisms, repartee and jump suits, he has brought his hero back to life.

The people who come to see Ben perform know that he is not Elvis, but they want to believe that he is, and he does everything he can to indulge them. 'A show is won or lost by the time you get to the microphone,' he says. It isn't enough for a tribute act to sing like Elvis; they must dress, behave and move like him. 'I'm trying to help them relive a moment, to imagine what it would have been like. I think they see it as a chance to see something they wish they'd seen the first time around.' As Elvis, Ben needs the fans as much as they need him. 'They have a massive part to play. I give them a show, and I expect a show back. It's fifty–fifty. The more energetic they are, the more they scream for every move, the more inspired I become. It's a harmonious circle.' It could have been Elvis talking – in a South London accent.[19]

———

Imitation is a powerful way to keep alive the memory of a star who has died. It can also help resurrect a group that has disbanded.

In August 2019, I joined thousands of fans at the annual Beatles Convention in Liverpool's Adelphi Hotel, an event that first took place in 1977. It was everything you'd expect of a week-long celebration of the Beatles: a mix of nostalgia, trivia and joy. There was the predictable merchandise, the manna of Beatlemania: old concert tickets, promotional posters, vinyl picture discs, a 'Yellow Submarine' toy bus, inflatable dolls of John, Paul, George and Ringo, autographs (I could have bought all four for £6,000) and 'the only authentic Beatles wig' (a snip at £170). Meanwhile, in an enormous ballroom, a succession of figures from the Beatles' past – an early manager, a session musician, one of Ringo's producers – entertained a reverential audience with stories they had likely heard before. Many of the fans were repeat visitors: I met a forty-nine-year-old Liverpudlian, Simon Noble, who had been every year since he was twelve. 'I was at the second ever convention, in 1981, and it has got bigger and bigger each year. The fan base just seems to grow. Look at all the young people here.'

The memorabilia stands and the parade of luminaries were well attended, but as it turned out they were really a side show. The biggest draw – the part everyone had come to see – were the tribute acts. Winning a slot as a tribute act at the Beatles Convention is no mean feat. You're up against groups from across the world: the 2019 line-up included bands from Mexico, Finland, Sweden, Spain, Canada, Argentina, Brazil, Serbia, Colombia, Norway, Italy, Hungary and Guatemala. It was hard not to be mesmerized by the five-piece from Indonesia wearing red, blue and gold Sergeant Pepper-style jackets, or the all-female group from Japan sporting red lipstick and identical mop tops. Many of the acts make a living imitating the Beatles, even though none of them were alive when the band was together.

You don't win plaudits as a tribute band by being idiosyncratic. The most popular looked and sounded exactly like the Beatles, which allowed the audience to imagine that they were watching the real thing. I arrived at the concert hall as a Dutch act called the Beatles Sessions were delivering an energetic rendition of 'Penny Lane'. It was scrupulously faithful to the original and to the Beatles' youthful optimism. The audience seemed caught between rapture and melancholy, as if calling to mind a happy memory they didn't want to let go. Outside, I asked a Glaswegian couple, Billy and Sandra Madden, what the music meant to them. They had grown up in the 1960s, and the Beatles provided the soundtrack to their youth, they said. The songs acted as memory markers for the things that had happened to them and the people they had met. They never got to see the Beatles play live, but this was their twenty-first convention. Another fan, Jane Blokland, told me it was her twenty-sixth; she hadn't missed one since her first in 1994. She wore a thigh-length tie-dye singlet imprinted with an image of the Beatles and it was clear the band's fifty-year hiatus had not dimmed her love for them. She called the convention a 'grand reunion'; she saw the same people here every year, and then she saw them again at the tribute gigs she attended over the months that followed.

The Beatles Sessions were a sensation, appreciated equally by the teenagers dancing at the front and the old-timers reminiscing at the back. Matthijs Klein, the band's twenty-two-year-old singer, seemed a little bemused by the attention. 'We're not used to people asking us for our autographs or taking pictures with us,' he said. 'We're nobody.' Of course, as everyone here knows, that isn't quite true. When the Beatles Sessions are on stage in their dark suits and ties playing 'All You Need Is Love' and the whole room is singing along, nobody is in any doubt who they are. And they aren't from the Netherlands.[20]

––––––

The adoration of the Beatles when they emerged onto the scene in the early 1960s was unlike anything that had gone before. Don Short, the journalist who coined the term 'Beatlemania',[21] says the atmosphere at their gigs at the Cavern Club in Liverpool before they were widely known was already 'pretty frenetic'. It soon escalated. Short came up with 'Beatlemania' after a concert in Cheltenham in 1963 during their first headline tour. He recalls, 'The fans were making so much noise it was unbelievable – screaming, shouting, waving, all of them out of their seats. The Beatles were breaking the rulebook, and the fans liked that. A lot of people thought the newspapers made the Beatles, but that's nonsense – it was the fans.'[22]

The majority of Beatles fans in the 1960s were teenage girls. They were widely derided for their unrestrained passion, and particularly for their habit of screaming during concerts. Screaming provided the backdrop to every public appearance the group made from 1963 until their final concert at Candlestick Park in San Francisco on 29 August 1966 – on many occasions they were unable to hear themselves play. Journalists denounced the fans as mindless and their behaviour as an affliction. 'Those who flock round the Beatles, who scream themselves into hysteria, are the least fortunate of their generation, the dull, the idle, the failures,' huffed Paul Johnson in the *New Statesman* in 1964. 'Their existence, in such large numbers . . . is a fearful indictment of our education system, which in ten years of schooling can scarcely raise them to literacy.'[23]

With the benefit of hindsight, there's another way to interpret the behaviour of these young fans: as a revolution, the first orchestrated almost entirely by young women. One gender-based analysis of Beatlemania called it 'a riot against the adult world', an attempt by teenage girls to break out of the sexual repression of the early 1960s and the expectations of their parents that they would be chaste and virtuous until marriage. 'When the screams drowned out the music, as they invariably did, then it was the fans, and not the band, who were the show.'[24] By this assessment, the Beatles' young female fans loved them not just for their music, but for what they appeared to stand for: freedom, independence, playfulness and rebellion.

Half a century later, the same sneers and insults were being levelled at teenage fans of One Direction. Like Beatles fans,

'Directioners' were known for their uninhibited enthusiasms, which included screaming, and these affectations upset the critics just as they had in the 1960s. In 2015, the men's magazine GQ described the audience at a One Direction concert as 'an ocean of 20,000 wide-open mouths, hundreds of pleading white eyes, 40,000 palms raised skywards, a dark-pink oil slick that howls and moans and undulates with every impish crotch-thrust from their idols' plinths'.[25] The writer, a thirty-four-year-old man, admitted that he had left the gig early, complaining about what he called 'the shrill sonic boom of a whole generation of women coming of age'. He had made a common ethnographic error in trying to judge the norms of an in-group by contemplating it from the outside. The first impulse of those who don't understand a culture has often been to rage against it.

Screaming is a collective act as well as an emotional one, a clan ritual that subverts the established order. It carries a powerful sense of belonging: nobody screams alone. Mark Duffett, who researches popular music fandoms at the University of Chester, recognizes it as an expression of political freedom: 'The female fans who scream own not just their heroes, but their collective right to emotionally express that sense of ownership.'[26] It may not feel quite like that at the time. In her book about the One Direction fandom, *Everything I Need I Get From You*, Kaitlyn Tiffany reflects on why she used to scream at their concerts, and what that 'rough and loud' experience represented, if anything. She eventually settles on this: 'We knew that our lives would not be fantasies, except for the fact that they were right now. When we shrieked, it was at the knowledge that the moment would end.'[27]

If the critics don't get it, the stars themselves often do. Paul McCartney once pointed out that teenage Beatles fans were not so different to football fans in the way they expressed themselves: 'If you go to a football match, a big FA Cup Final, you'll see all the men going, "Aaaaaaahhh!" This is the girls' equivalent.'[28] And in 2017, One Direction singer Harry Styles forever endeared himself to his teenage-girl fans when he told *Rolling Stone* magazine:

Who's to say that young girls who like pop music – short for popular, right? – have worse musical taste than a thirty-year-old hipster guy? That's not up to you to say. Music is something that's always changing. There's no goal posts. Young girls like the Beatles. You going to tell me they're not serious? How can you say young girls don't get it? They're our future. Our future doctors, lawyers, mothers, presidents, they kind of keep the world going. Teenage-girl fans – they don't lie. If they like you, they're *there*.[29]

———

Euphoric reactions to the presence of a celebrity are extremely common. By contrast, pathological obsessiveness – known as 'compulsive consumption' by psychologists – is rare, though it gets a disproportionate amount of media attention, thanks to the extravagances of a few deluded fans, such as the one who set her sights on Dave Garroway.

Garroway, the American television presenter and founding host of NBC's *Today* show, had many female admirers, though none of them as persistent as the woman who turned up one day in Chicago where he lived and booked herself into a big hotel, pretending to be his wife. She opened several credit accounts in his name, and a joint bank account into which she deposited a large sum of money. A few weeks later, she took a taxi to Garroway's hotel and informed the receptionist that she was moving in.[30]

Garroway frequently received letters from people who believed that he was addressing them directly through his chatty and intimate broadcasts. Although he found some of his fans difficult to deal with, none of them appeared to be ill. His fake wife was an exception. She had constructed a parasocial relationship with the presenter that defied objective reality. Cases such as this tend not to end well – it can be hard to convince a delusional person that they have a problem – but 'Mrs Dave Garroway' was eventually persuaded to return home.

It's surprising that mental illness is not more common in fandoms. Being in a relationship with someone who doesn't have a clue who you are can be challenging even for those who remain fully functional. 'These relationships can be enjoyable and real in certain ways that count . . . but talking to someone who will not talk back can also make you feel like you're losing your mind,' said Kaitlyn Tiffany, who as well as following One Direction has been very open about her fondness for the Hollywood actor Jake Gyllenhaal.[31] For a year, she wrote a weekly newsletter about him. Though she describes herself as 'obsessive', she manages to be self-deprecating and funny, a good tactic for keeping her interest healthy:

Does Jake Gyllenhaal know I'm in this room? This is a question I ask myself about 40 times a day, because I guess I just sort of assume that wherever Jake Gyllenhaal is, he's working hard to figure out what I'm doing.[32]

The trouble begins when fans who are unhappy or depressed cast their favourite star as their saviour, a Messiah figure they think will be able to redeem them. This is, of course, a catastrophic strategy – the star cannot fulfil this role and likely is not even aware that the person exists. In their collection of fan material from the 1980s, Fred and Judy Vermorel included nineteen letters written by a young woman named Cheryl to the singer-songwriter Nick Heyward over the course of a single month. Cheryl was very unhappy, and she had fixated on Heyward as the one who would turn that around. Here's a taste:

12 September
Dear Nick,
Will you please meet me on the 23rd? I really need to talk to you. I don't know why, but somehow I think you'll understand what I mean, more than anyone else around me.

22 September
Dear Nick,
Well, tomorrow's the day of truth. Will you be there? I don't think so somehow. I live in hope though.

23 September
Dear Nick,
You didn't turn up. I knew you wouldn't, but it still hurts. It was just today that kept me going, hoping that I might get to meet you. I've got no one else I can turn to.[33]

Shortly after sending this last letter, Cheryl went into a severe depression and tried to take her own life. By the time the

Vermorels published their work seven months later, she was in recovery, though apparently 'still deeply in love with Nick'.[34]

While most celebrities are careful to protect themselves from the excesses of fandom, the demands of their most persistent fans can be hard to deal with. Recently, Nancy Baym, a communications scholar at Microsoft Research, interviewed dozens of well-known performers for a study on the interaction between musicians and their audiences.[35] Nearly all her subjects, who included Billy Bragg, Lloyd Cole, Kristin Hersh from the rock band Throwing Muses and Roger O'Donnell, keyboard player in The Cure, told her that a small number of fans assume the relationship is mutual and mistake their adulation for friendship. This false intimacy can be unsettling; it is hard for performers to strike a balance. They can try to distance themselves from fans who communicate too much or with too much intensity, but they often rely on the familiarity of social media to keep their audiences close, resulting in mixed messages. Fans love being party to their idols' private lives. Those who follow Ariana Grande on Instagram will have seen her feeding pizza to her dog or modelling a dress in her home. Katy Perry, who has a bigger audience on Twitter than any other woman, is well known for opening up to her followers in this way. On a typical occasion a while back, she tweeted twelve times over the course of a week, offering titbits of personal information such as her love of tacos, her delight at cherry trees coming into blossom and her support for a presidential candidate.[36] Most fans revel in such intimacies; for a few, it can lead to a morbid fixation.

Where does the boundary lie between healthy and excessive adoration? Researchers have been trying to answer this question for several decades. Around twenty years ago, a group of psychologists led by John Maltby at the University of Leicester and Lynn McCutcheon of the *North American Journal of Psychology* developed a questionnaire called the Celebrity Attitude Scale,[37] which is used to assess the intensity of people's feelings for celebrities. Most fans fit into one of three categories: entertainment-social (they're mostly in it for the fun), intense-personal (the more serious fans) or borderline-pathological (those whose interest has become dysfunctional).[38] Where you are on this spectrum depends on how you respond to the thirty-four statements in the questionnaire. Fun-loving fans, for example, would be expected to agree most strongly with anodyne statements such as 'My friends and I like to discuss what my favorite celebrity has done' and 'I enjoy watching, reading or listening to my favourite celebrity because it means a good time'. Those who feel an intense personal attachment to their star would score highly on the likes of 'I am obsessed by details of my favorite celebrity's life' and 'I consider my favorite celebrity to be my soulmate'. If you give the thumbs up to any of the following, you are probably at the extreme end of the scale: 'I would gladly die in order to save the life of my favorite celebrity', 'If I were lucky enough to meet my favorite celebrity and he/she asked me to do something illegal as a favor, I would probably do it' and 'If I walked through the door of my favorite celebrity's home without an invitation, she or he would be happy to see me'.

Borderline-pathological fans often have seriously impaired psychological functioning. Researchers including Maltby and McCutcheon have found that as well as being at high risk of anxiety, depression and obsessive-compulsive disorder, their tendency to fantasize eventually causes them to become detached from reality.[39] Once they have entered that wormhole, they get drawn further and further from the light, consumed by their addiction to a fantastical relationship.[40] In some cases, their dissociation and obsession can cause them to become violent.

In September 1996, a twenty-one-year-old Uruguayan-American man called Ricardo López sent a letter-bomb containing sulphuric acid to the singer Björk, aiming to disfigure or kill her. After mailing the package, López returned to his apartment in Hollywood, Florida, and took his own life. Four days later, police broke into his home and discovered his decomposing body, along with a diary and twenty-two hours of video tape. They watched the tape, learned of his plan and contacted detectives at Scotland Yard in London, who intercepted the bomb before it reached Björk's home.

Afterwards, the psychologist Louis Schlesinger analysed López's diary to try to understand what had led him to such a desperate act, a process known as a psychological autopsy. Schlesinger discovered a personality and state of mind completely at odds with what López's family and friends knew of him. In the diary, López described feeling profoundly inadequate, referring to himself as 'a loser who never learned to drive . . . I don't respect myself . . . I never held a girl in my arms [and have never been] loved or even liked by a girl . . . [I feel] completely alone . . . Someone said I smell like a dog . . . You can't begin to realize how weird I feel.' Over the course of 803 pages, he mentioned Björk 408 times. He described her as 'so angelic, elegant and sweet', adding, 'I couldn't have sex with her because I love her.' He desperately wanted to 'have an effect on her life', and to play an important part in it. He even fantasized about travelling back to the mid-1970s to befriend her family and become involved in her upbringing. But his attitude towards her changed when he discovered that she had become involved with the musician Goldie, a mixed-race relationship he considered unacceptable. 'I wasted eight months and she had a fucking lover,' he wrote. He felt angry and betrayed; fifteen months later, he mailed his bomb.[41]

It is common for dysfunctional fans like López to develop impossible fantasies about their relationship with their idol or the role they dream of playing in their lives. As well as being delusional, they differ from other fans in another important respect: they tend to be socially isolated. Fandoms are inherently social – often joyously so – which accounts for many of the psychological benefits they bring. One of the incentives for being part of a fandom is that you get to do things with others. You might go to the same gigs, or rave together on social media about an artist's new album. At the extreme end of the scale, the opposite is true. Pathological fans are inherently anti-social. They hunt alone, and their isolation fuels their dysfunctionality, since they have no one to temper their fantasies or the appropriateness of their emotions. In the two years before his death, Ricardo López became increasingly reclusive, and none of his acquaintances were aware of the extent of his obsession with Björk or the troubled state of his mind. Eric Swarbrick, one of dozens of stalkers who have targeted Taylor Swift, began trying to contact the singer after he became convinced that she had reached out to him in his dreams. Over four years he sent her more than forty letters and emails – some of them containing death threats – and on three occasions he drove nine hundred miles from his home in Austin, Texas, to deliver them in person. A friend might have persuaded him that his behaviour was improper, but his only confidante was the voice in his head.

The behaviour of some stalker fans can be devastating for their victims. A year after López's death, Björk told the *Guardian* journalist Lindsay Baker: 'I was very upset that somebody had died. I couldn't sleep for a week. And I'd be lying if I said it didn't scare the fuck out of me. That I could get hurt and, most of all, that my son could get hurt.'[42] The singer-songwriter Lily Allen was pursued for seven years by a man who believed, among many other delusions, that he had written one of her songs. He sent her threatening letters and aggressively trolled her on social media. Then one night he broke into her home and confronted her in her bedroom. He was arrested and later detained indefinitely under the Mental Health Act, but Allen is scared of what he might do should he ever be released. 'It affected me hugely,' she wrote in her autobiography. 'It violated every area of my psyche. It made me feel scared and paranoid.'[43]

———

The enthusiastic attention of fans can be disconcerting for artists even if it isn't directly threatening. The British band Gay Dad experienced a dramatic rise to fame in the late 1990s after the music press touted them as the saviours of British pop. They featured on the cover of several magazines and were the first act to perform on the BBC chart show *Top of the Pops* before they'd even released a record. Their lead singer, Cliff Jones, says what they went through was 'like a tsunami. You could feel this thing coming towards you, and then our feet didn't touch the ground for two or three years. Nobody can prepare you for it.' His interactions with fans were generally positive, though they occasionally felt spectacularly weird. He remembers one fan presenting him with a large cake after every gig, and another who regularly found his way backstage and insisted on addressing him by his surname while refusing to make eye contact. On returning to London from a tour of Japan in 1999, Jones entered his flat to find that two female fans had broken in, taken Polaroids of themselves and left them on his bed. He received a lot of fan fiction depicting him in various fantasy scenarios, some of them sexual, some of them with him and his bandmates cast as super-heroes – 'that felt a bit *too* weird,' he says.

Today, as well as writing and producing music, Jones researches and lectures in social theory – including fan behaviour – at Bath Spa University, a role that has helped him reflect on his experience with Gay Dad and, more generally, the relationship between artists and their audiences. He says it is crucial for an artist to realize that they can never control their public persona, which is based not so much on who they are but on what their fans want from them. 'As a performer you have to accept that what other people think about you is as valid as what you think about your-self. You provide a social function: you become a cipher for a set of values or ideas that they may wish to share or embody as a group. What's damaging for artists is when they take that ser-iously and push back and say, no, I'm not like that. It's easier to give the fans some of what they need, because at some point you have to admit that you are complicit in it. I didn't really understand that until it was too late.'

Some artists use the term 'psychic vampires' when describing their most persistent fans, referring to their tendency to relent-lessly feed on whatever it is they think they need from them. In the late 2000s, I played in a band with a singer who had a knack for attracting psychic vampires. Her stage name was Lizzyspit – she was also a solo artist in her own right – and at each of our gigs she would point out various members of the audience who turned up wherever she performed. We tended to play in obscure, out-of-the-way London clubs, and she was always curious how these fans tracked her down. They were usually middle-aged men who would stand on their own in the small crowd, staring at her. She didn't seem too bothered by them, but they certainly freaked me out.

Lizzyspit went on to become one of the most popular solo artists on Google+, a social network that operated between 2011 and 2019. In early 2011 she moved to a small town in Western Australia and, lacking a local audience, played an online gig for her friends via the Google+ Hangouts video platform. Her friends shared the video with their friends, who shared it with *their* friends, and within a few days Lizzyspit had 4,000 followers. Over the next month that grew to 16,000, and after a year it was approaching a million. Google saw what was happening and started promoting her as one of their global influencers. By the end of 2013, she had nearly three million followers on the platform, and around 10,000 more on YouTube, Facebook and Twitter. But her popularity came at a considerable cost.

Each time Lizzyspit posted something online, she received hundreds of comments. Most of them were positive and supportive, though some were vicious. She had a group of super-fans who called themselves the Spits, and at least two of them had lyrics from her songs tattooed on their arms. A few would almost certainly fit into the borderline-pathological category of Maltby and McCutcheon's Celebrity Attitude Scale. They demanded special attention from her, and were offended when they didn't receive it. 'I felt grateful, but also like they owned me,' she told me. 'And if I didn't put stuff out there, they'd have a go at me. There was a time when I lost my dad and ended up being offline for about six weeks. I came back online to sort of apologise, and the first comment was, "You think you're so much better than us, you can't even be bothered to update us about your life." That was when I thought, "Oh my god, what am I in?"'

The worst abuse came from a small number of male fans who became outraged when she tried to distance herself from the online discourse. They started a campaign to encourage people to vote against her in the Shorty Awards, which honours creators of short-form content on social media. They set up a web page where they discussed how they might kill her, and one of them even contacted her mother to vent his hate. She received multiple death and rape threats, and many pictures of male genitalia. Someone sent her a photograph of the back of her own head with the message, 'I was behind you today. I didn't say hi, but I was there.' She lost count of the number of times she was called a whore or accused of sleeping her way to the top.

Lizzyspit's songs are heartfelt and relatable. All fans crave authenticity, and that's what they get from her. She gives the impression that she's allowing you access to her soul, which leaves her vulnerable to both love and criticism. Unlike most of today's social media influencers, she had no corporate shield to protect her from fandom's intemperance. The psychic vampires could feast where they pleased. Social media had developed to a point where stars and fans were able to interact like never before. People gave more, and they expected more in return. Lizzyspit's online fans had helped to make her a star. Was it a reasonable payoff?

Ultimately, she decided that it wasn't. 'It was making me anxious, it was depressing me,' she says. 'The vast majority of fans were genuinely nice and normal, but that weird group of two hundred or so became twisted and psychopathic. I became caught up on the idea of needing to please people. I remember having panic attacks when I couldn't get wi-fi to send something out. In the end I couldn't cope with it, I couldn't tolerate what was happening to me.'

In 2016, Lizzyspit's mother died, and she took another break from social media. When she logged back on, she found a message from a fan whose dog was apparently obsessed with her songs. This woman had sent a number of pictures and videos of the dog, and when Lizzyspit hadn't replied she accused her of being heartless and not caring about the people who made her. The next day, 16 December 2016, Lizzyspit closed all her social media accounts and deleted her blog. 'I decided I wasn't going to do it anymore. I deleted all my followers. I deleted everything. That was the end of my online music life.'

Despite the negative impact this decision had on her musical career, she has never regretted it – it was the only way to protect herself from the fans who had become pathologically dependent on her. 'I felt that as long as they had access to me in any way, I'd never truly be free of them.' She still lives with a small fear that they will find her. Recently one of them visited her LinkedIn profile, which is in her real name. 'I nearly had a panic attack,' she says. 'I was scared. I know who they are. I know they're still out there.'[44]

———

Pathological dependency aside, celebrity fandoms have much in common with other fandoms, particularly in their group dynamics and their collective psychology. Yet every fandom relates to the wider world in its own particular way. In the next two chapters, we'll be looking at two fandoms that inhabit quite separate places in the cultural landscape. One of them dates back two hundred years and is publicly celebrated by millions. The other is relatively recent, has a membership of hundreds and is largely invisible to anyone who doesn't know it exists.

5

Something about Jane

UNDER NORMAL CIRCUMSTANCES, WALKING through the streets of an English town in a bonnet and a full-length gown would invite mirth, mockery or even a hurled egg. When the town is Bath, capital of Regency style, and five hundred others similarly dressed are walking alongside you, there is little to fear, except perhaps the possibility of stepping on the hem of the person ahead.

Each September, the Grand Regency Costumed Promenade marks the start of Bath's Jane Austen Festival. Austen lived in Bath for six years and two of her novels are set here,[1] though (whisper it) she didn't like the place very much:

> Bath, compared with London, has little variety, and so everybody finds out every year. 'For six weeks I allow Bath is pleasant enough; but beyond that, it is the most tiresome place in the world.' You would be told so by people of all descriptions. (Henry Tilney to Catherine Morland, *Northanger Abbey*)[2]

In 2019 I joined in the festivities, though not, I'm ashamed to say, in Regency drag. The promenaders, unaware of or indifferent to Austen's slight, shuffled merrily through the stately streets, led by a town crier, a dance troupe and a company of red-coated infantry. I was there to ask the participants a few questions, and to find out how exactly they had reached this point in their lives.

Many of those taking part had made their own costumes or had them made by friends or family. Immaculately turned out, their main objective was to scrutinize everyone else's get-up for authenticity and craftsmanship. 'It's so competitive. Everybody's looking at other people's dresses thinking, "Is it hired? Have they made it themselves?"' observed Debbie Willcox from Worthing. She was promenading in Georgian attire with her brother, mother, son and daughter.[3] She had been dressing up her family like this for thirty years. Lately she had found fresh inspiration in the Instagram feed of a group of cosplayers called the Jane Austen Pineapple Appreciation Society. I would hear a lot about them before the day was out.

While Bath's annual promenade is on, you cannot move in the city for dresses, bonnets, shawls, tailcoats, waistcoats, cravats, felt hats, fans, walking canes, pantaloons and parasols. I spotted some familiar characters from Jane Austen's life and novels, including Mr Darcy, the haughty hero of *Pride and Prejudice*, his sparring partner Elizabeth Bennet and the Dashwood sisters from *Sense and Sensibility*. Outside the Guildhall I bumped into Mr Collins, the obsequious clergyman from *Pride and Prejudice*, hard to miss in his clerical cravat and black felt hat. In his other life he is Jonathan Engberg of Oregon, and he had travelled five thousand miles with his wife and two young daughters especially for this festival. They were parading as the Collins family, though the daughters let slip that they would have preferred to cosplay as

Emma Woodhouse and her governess Miss Taylor from *Emma*. 'Jane Austen was an amazing observer of human nature,' said Jonathan. 'You can find her characters wherever you go.' As we shuffled on, an onlooker called out, 'Bless me, Father!', and he duly obliged.

People connect with Jane Austen in myriad ways. Plenty of those taking part in the promenade hadn't read her books. Many of them knew her novels through film and television adaptations, particularly the BBC's popular 1995 production of *Pride and Prejudice* which – thanks to a (completely made-up) scene featuring Colin Firth in a wet shirt – doubled the size of the fandom overnight. The true adoring fans, who call themselves Janeites,[4] are hard to pick out among the elaborately dressed crowd, but you know them when you meet them. Their fascination with Austen is deep-set.

The Jane Austen Pineapple Appreciation Society represents a modern breed of Janeite. Their Instagram feed shows one or more of them in Regency finery as they take their leisure: foraging in the woods, admiring a rose garden, drinking tea on a terrace or gazing over a lake. Sometimes the photographs are overprinted with an Austen quote, such as 'A little harmless flirtation or so will occur' (*Northanger Abbey*) or 'Good company is always worth seeking' (*Persuasion*). I caught up with them at the Promenader's Fayre inside the Guildhall, where one of them was signing copies of her book (on Jane Austen, of course). They were attracting considerable interest; it was hard to get a look-in. I would get to know a few of them quite well over the months to come, but for now it seemed best to leave them to the attentions of their own fans.

———

More than two hundred years after her death from lupus[5] in 1817 at the age of forty-one, Jane Austen is one of the best known and most widely loved novelists in the English language. But during her lifetime she was relatively anonymous, and remained so until 1869, when her nephew James Edward Austen-Leigh published *A Memoir of Jane Austen*, a biography of his 'dear Aunt Jane' that brought her to the notice of the wider public.[6] Suddenly everyone wanted to learn about this amateur author with a 'prolific mind' and an 'unusually quick sense of the ridiculous'.[7] A few years later, the publisher George Routledge and Sons reissued her novels in a set of affordable editions for the mass market. Literary critics had already begun to take her seriously, though not all were comfortable with her growing popularity. Leslie Stephen, the father of Virginia Woolf and Vanessa Bell, decried what he called 'Austenolatry' as 'perhaps the most intolerant and dogmatic of literary creeds',[8] a reference to the fervour with which Austen enthusiasts defended her literary merits.

Austen's fandom looked a little different then to how it looks today – more male, more elitist – but since the 1870s it has never really waned. In a much-cited essay published to commemorate the centenary of her death, the travel writer and intellectual Reginald Farrer described her following as 'a cult as ardent as a religion'. He went on: 'In water-logged trench, in cold cave of the mountains, in sickness and in health, in dulness [sic], tribulation and fatigue, an ever-increasing crowd of worshippers flies insatiably for comfort and company' to the country houses and communities of her novels.[9]

Farrer's 'water-logged trench' is a reference to one of Austen's most unlikely fan groups: British soldiers during the First World War, who read her to remind themselves of the England they were fighting for. Rudyard Kipling found comfort in reading Austen to his family after the death in action of his son John; his short story 'The Janeites', published in 1924, describes a secret society of British soldiers on the Western Front who trade quotations from her novels to distract themselves from the horrors around them.[10] Farrer in his essay described Austen as 'comparable only to Shakespeare' in her ability to project universal truths about humanity onto particular characters, and this is evidently one of the qualities that makes it easy for such a broad mix of groups to appreciate her, from literary critics to soldiers, from feminist theorists to Regency cosplayers. Her novels have become a staple of both high culture and pop culture.

Modern fans of Jane Austen have endless ways to share their love. They can join their national Jane Austen Society (most countries seem to have one) or contribute to the discussion at the Republic of Pemberley online community (sample topic: 'Is Wentworth's letter to Anne in *Persuasion* the most romantic thing ever written?'). They can read a blog by another Janeite or start their own. They can wear a T-shirt inscribed with a quotation from one of her books or attend a symposium on the use of irony in *Mansfield Park*. Or they can dive into the multiple parallel universes of Jane Austen fan fiction.

In December 2020, I joined 231 Janeites at a virtual tea party organized by Jane Austen's House Museum in Chawton, Hampshire, to celebrate the author's 245th birthday. Fans of all ages logged on from Brazil, the Philippines, Australia, Japan, Italy, Belgium, Croatia, the Czech Republic, Sweden, France, Germany, the Netherlands, Ireland, Canada, America and all over the UK. Among the 231, I counted just five men (myself included) and one person of colour. Most of the participants were in their sitting rooms, sipping from porcelain mugs. Many wore bonnets (there was a 'best bonnet' competition). One mother and her daughter were dressed in full Regency. A lady from Hampshire knitted throughout.

It was an occasion of quaint delight. While we took our tea, the organizers entertained us with a lesson on how to make spiced orange wine (a Regency tipple), a reading from *Pride and Prejudice* and a lecture about what Regency folk wore in winter. There followed a group singalong to 'Happy Birthday', a discordant jamboree. The party ended with a quiz, which gave everyone the chance to show off their Janeite credentials. 'How many of Austen's novels were published during her lifetime (four)?' 'What was her working title for *Pride and Prejudice* (*First Impressions*)?' 'Who was she engaged to for just one night (Harris Bigg-Wither)?' Each question was answered in seconds.

We signed off with a group wave and a chorus of 'We love you Jane!', a salutation that defines one way in which Janeites differ from other fandoms that celebrate fictional worlds. Janeites love her characters, her novels and the milieux they inhabit, but they feel a particular affection for her as a person. They treat her like a friend, with easy familiarity: they're on first-name terms. In the early twentieth century, Jane Austen fans were referred to as Austenites, but the term never really caught on. It sounded too formal. It had to be Jane.

———

The Jane Austen Pineapple Appreciation Society (JAPAS) is unusual among Janeite groups: in a fandom that is skewed towards middle-age, its members are all in their twenties and thirties. The founders came together in September 2015 after meeting at successive Bath festivals and deciding that once a year was not enough. The first get-together was a week-long house party of the type that happens in every Austen novel: tea was taken, dresses were worn, games were played. The house party has since become an annual event, part of a calendar of Austen-related engagements – picnics, musical soirees, Regency balls, excursions to National Trust houses – that fill the months between March and September. JAPAS has around twenty active members. They don't worry too much about historical accuracy and are all for mixing Jane Austen with their other passions: they've hosted a Regency–Harry Potter crossover day, and a Regency ball with a Disney twist. They celebrate Jane Austen with fun, and they're fairly sure Jane would approve. Pineapples, in case you're wondering, were a status symbol in the Regency era, appreciated in the finest houses. (Because they were imported from the Caribbean, they have also come to represent Britain's oppressive colonial history. Since December 2020, JAPAS has been engaging in an on-going conversation on its social media feeds about the use of the pineapple and the origins of white wealth in the early nineteenth century.)

The chief organizer of JAPAS and its most visible ambassador is twenty-six-year-old Sophie Andrews, a self-described 'Jane Austen specialist and devotee'. Sophie started reading Austen when she was sixteen, at a difficult time in her life. Her sister and father had both been seriously ill, and she was suffering from ill-health herself. She was also finding it difficult to fit in with her peer group at school, not sharing their enthusiasm for drinking, clubbing, make-up and boys. Her English teacher encouraged her to read *Pride and Prejudice*, and she fell hard for the eloquence of Austen's language and the elegance of her world. She read her other novels, and she kept falling. 'Jane Austen became an escape for me,' she says. 'I threw myself into her stories. They made me happy, because good things happen to good people there. As Jane herself said, "Let other pens dwell on guilt and misery." Compared with what was going on in my real life, I had found somewhere I felt comfortable and safe.'

Sophie began to identify with Elizabeth Bennet, the independent-minded heroine of *Pride and Prejudice* (she now owns more than a hundred different editions of this novel). She respected Lizzie's irreverence, her determination to speak her mind, her refusal to be cowed by status or convention, and her habit of going for muddy walks by herself despite her mother's disapproval. 'Those are all admirable traits, even now. There is so much peer pressure today: this is how you should look, this is what you should do. It can be hard not to go along with the crowd. Lizzie never let other people tell her what to do.' When she was sixteen, Sophie started a blog called 'Laughing with Lizzie', which she uses to 'spread the wit and wisdom of Jane Austen'; she has thirty thousand followers on social media.[11] Her recent book, *Be More Jane*, explores how Austen's novels and letters can help us cope with the challenges of twenty-first-century life; it includes lessons on self-belief, the role of women and how to avoid false friends. Times change, she says, but we still face the same problems.[12]

Sophie's connection with Lizzie Bennet is typical of parasocial relationships in other areas of popular culture. Identifying with fictional characters allows fans to explore values that they admire and to learn from role models who will never let them down. As a member of JAPAS, Sophie has discovered another thing common to all fandoms: the reassurance that comes from being part of a close-knit group. When Sophie began reading Jane Austen, she felt like she was her only fan. It came as a revelation to discover on the internet that the author was so universally beloved. 'It was such a sense of relief to know that there were other people like me, and that I could talk to them endlessly about Jane Austen without boring them,' she says. She began to attend events and to meet other fans in person, a process that led to the founding of JAPAS. 'The Pineapples', as she calls them, are now her core friendship group, 'a place where you can be yourself without fear of judgement' – not to mention wear a bonnet without having to explain why.

Sophie's story of suffering, isolation and redemption is surprisingly common among Janeites. Many people in times of hardship have found refuge in Austen, including those shell-shocked soldiers on the Western Front, and J. K. Rowling, who has spoken about drawing comfort from her novels during a period of depression. Sophie's friend and fellow Pineapple Amy Coombes, who posts on social media as DressingMissDashwood, endured a long period of mental ill-health before she stumbled on JAPAS. 'The group has been such a massive part of my journey to getting back to a better place,' Amy says. 'Finding people of a similar age to me who completely geek out over Jane Austen and period dramas and pretty dresses was like, "Oh my gosh, I've finally found my people."'

That's the thing about Austen fan culture. You may not know it exists unless you're in it, but once you're in it, it can change your life.

Jane Austen's novels are concerned with a very thin slice of British society, though you don't have to be part of that land-owning elite to appreciate her work. Literary critics have for years contorted themselves trying to understand why she appeals to so broad an audience. Is it her acerbic wit? Her flawed characters? Her perfect sentences? Her romantic sensibilities? One answer is that her stories are open to interpretation. She makes it easy for us to import our own prejudices and motivations, to see our world in hers.

It is difficult to tell what Jane actually thought about what she was writing. Was she a satirist, a conservative, a feminist, a revolutionary? Did she admire the social world she was observing or disapprove of it? In *Among the Janeites: A Journey through the World of Jane Austen Fandom*, Deborah Yaffe – herself a devotee – suggests that Austen's fans invariably notice in her work a reflection of their own preoccupations. Feminists see independent-minded women who defy patriarchal conventions; Christians see a commitment to biblical values. But this diversity of responses does not mean that her stories are 'blank canvases onto which we project ourselves', says Yaffe. 'They are complicated, ambiguous pictures of lived reality. We all find ourselves in her because, in a sense, she contains us all.'[13]

Janeites sometimes appear conflicted about what they like about Austen. Sophie and Amy, along with their fellow Pineapples, are drawn to the elegance, good manners and civility that define her social worlds, while also rooting for the characters who challenge those conventions. There's nothing contradictory about that: Austen's radicals tend to be both independent-minded *and* polite. Sophie, along with many other Janeites, recognizes Elizabeth Bennet as a proto-feminist for the way she resists the patriarchal norms of her society without alienating herself from it. In the context of the period, it takes considerable courage to refuse both her cousin Mr Collins because he is a sanctimonious creep and the fabulously wealthy Mr Darcy because he seems conceited and selfish. We can take it from Austen that it pays to be courageous, since in marrying Darcy after re-assessing his character Lizzie ends up with both money and love.

Even Austen's quieter heroines get an opportunity to stand up against the forces that oppress them. Towards the end of *Persuasion*, Anne Elliot, who has lacked confidence for much of the novel, makes a stand during a debate with her friend Captain Harville on whether men or women are more loyal and long-lasting in love. Harville claims that all the books he has ever read speak of women's inconstancy and fickleness, whereupon Anne rebukes him with a lesson in social injustice. When she finds her voice, she is no less effective as a feminist hero than Lizzie Bennet.

For some Janeites, Austen's subversiveness extends beyond female empowerment to severe social criticism. They perceive beneath the propriety and civility a subtext of withering satire. One of the first to read Austen this way, the psychologist D. W. Harding, referred to this aspect of Austen's work as 'regulated hatred', suggesting that it was her intention to write books that could be 'read and enjoyed by precisely the sort of people whom she disliked; she is a literary classic of the society which attitudes like hers, held widely enough, would undermine.'[14]

We'll never know if this *was* Austen's intention, though there is plenty in her books to give us pause. She is quick to put down snobs, egoists, bootlickers, charlatans, hypochondriacs and other dubious characters, and to take issue with morally questionable decisions. In *Pride and Prejudice*, Mrs Bennet is introduced with no little spite as 'a woman of mean understanding, little information, and uncertain temper',[15] and remains unloved by her creator throughout. Equally caustic is the moral judgement that Austen has Elizabeth Bennet deliver against her friend Charlotte Lucas after she accepts Mr Collins as her husband. Read this way, Austen's work contains enough to interest fans who may be less enamoured of her depictions of etiquette and romance.[16]

———

Jane Austen's novels are famously rich in meaning and nuance of character. But for some Janeites, this isn't enough. They want her stories to go places Austen could never have taken them. Fans being fans, they're happy to do that work for her.

Jane Austen fan fiction has become a hugely profitable genre of publishing. *Pride and Prejudice* alone has inspired more than six hundred literary derivations, including *Bridget Jones's Diary*,[17] whose screen adaptation features Colin Firth as the rude and awkward 'Mark Darcy'; and *Pride and Prejudice and Zombies*,[18] which incorporates scenes of zombie mayhem into Austen's original plot (her book was 'just ripe for gore and senseless violence', according to the author, Seth Grahame-Smith).[19] Austenprose, a blog dedicated to 'Austenesque' fiction, reviews at least two new books a week.[20] Archive of Our Own, the online repository of fan fiction, lists some four thousand Jane Austen spin-offs, more than half of which are drawn from *Pride and Prejudice*.

A good number of these works explore the endless possibilities thrown up by the inscrutable demeanour of Austen's most eligible bachelor. Titles in this sub-genre include *What Would Mr Darcy Do?*,[21] *Mr Darcy's Forbidden Love*,[22] *Mr Darcy, Vampyre*,[23] *Snowbound with Darcy*[24] and *My Darcy Vibrates . . .*[25] Since the notorious wet-shirt scene in the BBC's 1995 adaptation, the allure of Darcy is less to do with his winsome personality and more, shall we say, biological. Most Janeites I have met admit that they find him irresistible. Few are immune to this circus. In 2010, biologists at the University of Liverpool named a mouse sex pheromone after him: darcin.[26]

Aside from the freedom it allows them to explore their own fantasies, one reason Janeites write derivative fiction is to play around with issues of sexuality, gender and race. It allows them to consider how Jane Austen's world might have looked had the ingredients been different – had Mr Darcy been gay, for example, or the social framework been a matriarchy. In one fan-fiction version of *Pride and Prejudice*, the author has switched the biological gender of all the main characters, so Darcy is a woman and all the Bennet sisters are men. In this new version, it is the men rather than the women who are constantly agitating for a ball or to meet the officers of the local militia.[27]

Reinvention allows fans to address the criticism that people of colour rarely feature in television and film adaptations of Austen's novels (the 2022 Netflix version of *Persuasion* is a notable exception). Traditionalists argue that her characters should be represented as white because they are white in her stories. Look closer, however, and it is not so clear-cut. While Austen described personalities, emotional states and social dynamics in great detail, she was never specific about appearances. Mr Darcy is admired for his 'fine, tall person, handsome features, noble mien', and Elizabeth Bennet for her 'fine eyes' and her 'light and pleasing' figure. In *Persuasion*, Anne Elliot is described as 'an extremely pretty girl, with gentleness, modesty, taste, and feeling', and her love interest, Frederick Wentworth, as 'a remarkably fine young man, with a great deal of intelligence, spirit and brilliancy'. These broad depictions allow us to imagine the characters how we like. They give creators and producers permission to inject diversity into Austen, something all fans are likely to welcome. Most Janeites think that Austen would have been politically progressive had she been alive today. She is believed to have held abolitionist views, for example, a radical position in her time when many in her society benefited from the profits of slavery.[28]

———

I live in Hampshire, the county in which Jane Austen was born, died and wrote all her books. It is a prime destination for Janeite pilgrims, who come in their thousands to pay their respects and feel a little closer to their literary hero. An hour's carriage ride from my home is the village of Steventon, where Austen's father was rector and she spent the first twenty-five years of her life. The parsonage in which they lived, and where she wrote the first drafts of *Sense and Sensibility*, *Pride and Prejudice* and *Northanger Abbey*, was demolished not long after they moved to Bath in 1801. Except for the field where it once stood and a lime tree that is believed to have been planted by her eldest brother James, the remaining major place of interest to her fans is the thirteenth-century church where the Reverend Austen ministered. The walls of the church carry numerous memorials to members of her family, and outside the front door stands a sixteenth-century English yew in which her father kept the key.

Still, these are meagre pickings. So little of Austen is left in Steventon that visitors tend to resort to fantasy, imagining her walking the muddy lanes, delivering food to her neighbours or listening to her father's sermons. Constance Hill, an early Austen biographer, who toured 'Austen-land' with her sister in 1901, conjured her up among the 'fruit-trees and flowers' in the parsonage garden, fancying that she caught 'a glimpse of two girlish forms moving among them – those of Jane Austen and her sister Cassandra'.[29]

Imagination allows literary pilgrims not only to reincarnate their heroes in the places where they lived, but to treat fictional events as real and imagine them happening in real places. Two of the more celebrated Austen pilgrims of this era were the English poet Lord Tennyson and Charles Darwin's son Francis, each of whom visited the coastal town of Lyme Regis to scout out some of the settings that feature in *Persuasion*. They were drawn in particular to a flight of steps on the harbour wall where Louisa Musgrove, in the novel, miscalculates a jump into Captain Wentworth's arms and falls on the pavement. While climbing the steps himself, Darwin reported that he 'quite suddenly and inexplicably fell down' and that a friend of his did the same, leading him to deduce that the real cause of Louisa's accident was Captain Wentworth losing his footing as she jumped. 'It had never seemed comprehensible that an active and capable man should miss so easy a catch,' he wrote, satisfied that he had solved this supposed mystery.[30]

Austen is always clear in her novels which counties the action takes place in; occasionally she includes real towns like Lyme Regis and Bath. Although her country houses and local geographies are fictitious, her realistic descriptions offer her fans plenty of clues as to where they might be – for example, Pemberley, Mr Darcy's home in *Pride and Prejudice*, is often imagined as Chatsworth House in Derbyshire. This abundance of material is enough to sustain a make-believe journey through Jane Austen's England without ever setting foot in Hampshire.

That would never do, of course. For most Janeites, the real draw is the life of Jane herself. Every year, the Jane Austen Society of North America (JASNA), which has more than five thousand members, organizes a tour of iconic Austen sites in England. The itinerary includes the church in Steventon; the family's house in Chawton, where she did much of her writing; Chawton House, the neighbouring manor house that belonged to her brother Edward; her grave in Winchester Cathedral; and various private homes with a connection to her life. I'm familiar with one of those homes, Ibthorpe House in Hampshire, as it used to belong to some close family friends. Austen's friend Martha Lloyd lived here during the 1790s, and Jane often stayed and worked on her novels in the guest bedroom on the first floor. I have slept in this room, as have various guests of the JASNA tours: for Janeites, this is as authentic as it gets. My friends recall hosting two couples who set their alarms for 3.30 a.m. so they could swap bedrooms to ensure that they each took a turn in Jane's room. They also recall a gentleman in rapture of Austen gripping the stairway banister while exclaiming, 'To think she laid her hand here!'[31]

Exhilaration is commonplace on JASNA visits. 'American tourists behave in a way that the English don't,' says Elizabeth Proudman, an Austen expert who led fifteen JASNA tours of the UK from the late 1990s. Elizabeth is a life-long Janeite; Austen's characters have been her 'friends' since she first read her novels as a schoolgirl. She is a former chair of the Jane Austen Society of the UK and she lives in Winchester – an Austen holy of holies – in a house with a view of the cathedral.

Elizabeth's JASNA tours drew college professors, doctors, CEOs, teachers, librarians, accountants and writers. Some of them toured in Georgian dress. 'They were incredibly well informed. You could ask them the name of Mrs Elton's sister [from *Emma*] and where she lived and they would all know. It was extraordinary. We would be together for ten days and we'd talk about Jane Austen all the time. That seems ridiculous, but there's so much to talk about.' The high point of the tour was a ceremony of remembrance at Austen's grave in Winchester Cathedral. A member of the clergy would read some prayers and the visitors would each lay a rose. 'And they would be crying,' says Elizabeth.

———

As Austen's final resting place, Winchester Cathedral draws many fans who want to reflect on her curtailed life. Some choose to pay their respects outside the house in which she died, a few hundred metres away on College Street. But neither Winchester nor her birthplace at Steventon is the most popular pilgrimage site. That accolade goes to the red-brick three-storey house in Chawton, seventeen miles east of Winchester, where she spent her last eight years and wrote or revised all six of her novels.

Sophie Andrews and Abigail Rose outside Jane Austen's house, Chawton, Hampshire. (Michael Bond)

The house opened as a museum in July 1949 and has become a place of celebration for Janeites. In typical years it receives around forty thousand visitors. It has a huge online following: around thirty thousand people subscribe to its Facebook page, where during the coronavirus pandemic it hosted tea parties, talks and a virtual walking tour of the house. Visitors to the museum often become deeply emotional, as if they were arriving at a holy place, or at a house of treasured childhood memories. Some have travelled thousands of miles to be there. I spent a day looking through the museum's eighty-six volumes of visitors' books, which date back to the day it was opened by the Duke of Wellington. A single page opened at random from March 2019 shows signatories from Western Australia, Virginia, London, South Wales, New York City, Madrid, Poland, Yorkshire, Japan, Hungary, Newcastle and Sri Lanka. Overleaf, someone has written, 'My beloved in India imagines herself to be out of a Jane Austen novel. It is for her that I come.'

Since 2002, the museum has permitted visitors to write comments. They do not disappoint:

A breathtaking, surreal experience. I still cannot believe I finally made it here. Her novels inspired my love for literature and set me on the path of becoming an English teacher, at a school where I teach her novels.

I have loved Jane for a very long time. Being here feels like stepping back in time – as I looked out her bedroom window, I felt captivated by her spirit.

My heroine since I was 14!

I was knitting all day in the garden and thoroughly enjoyed it.

Excellent. Very informative. Smells funny.

Many visitors wrote that they were 'ridiculously excited' to be there, that their visit was 'a dream come true' or that they had been 'waiting for years' to come. One woman asked if she could move in. Another, inspired by what she perceived to be Jane's presence, promised to name her daughter after her. A surprising number of people have proposed marriage in the house, at least three in the first three months of 2020. Others, committed Janeites, have taken the opportunity to address the author directly:

Oh Jane, you are dearly loved.

Thank you, Jane, for your beautiful works of art.

Beautiful Jane.

Jane, you changed my life.

Jane, you're the love of my life.

Visitors are often surprised by their own reaction to the house. They don't expect it to feel so authentic, or so much like a home. The trustees have been at pains to recreate the house that Austen lived in, reproducing some of the original wallpaper and filling the rooms with objects and furniture that the family owned. The effect is intimate and a little spooky. It is not hard to imagine her standing by her father at his bookcase or seated quill in hand at her writing table. For Janeites, it's the obvious place to resurrect her.

———

In September 2020, during a break in Britain's coronavirus lockdown, I visited Jane Austen's Chawton house with Sophie Andrews and Abigail Rose, another of Sophie's friends from JAPAS. Sophie has been so often that it feels almost as familiar as her own home. They both turned up in authentic Regency clothing: Sophie in a light-blue dress with flower motif, Abbie in gingham check. They wore elegant shawls draped over one shoulder and straw bonnets made by a friend. Their face masks, tastefully pleated and colour-matched, would have passed muster in a Regency pandemic. Anticipating their effort, I had put on a three-piece tweed suit, hardly of that era but at least not quite of this one.

It was a clear autumn day and we wandered for a while in the little garden at the back of the house. Sophie and Abbie attracted a lot of attention, which they were used to and, thankfully, enjoyed. 'I guess the people who think you're a complete weirdo don't talk to you, but you get so many who come and say, "You look amazing, did you make the dress yourself? Are you doing a play or something?" ' said Sophie. 'Everyone wants you to be in their picture.' Abbie, who despite her cheery disposition admits to being fairly reserved – an introspective Elinor Dashwood to Sophie's defiant Elizabeth Bennet – said she found her Regency costume empowering. 'It gives me confidence. It's actually easier to be confident in Regency clothes than it is in modern clothes, because you know what fits with the style and what goes with what.'

We stepped from the garden into the house, being careful to comply with a social distancing notice advising us to 'keep one Darcy apart'. Sophie and Abbie started discussing the wallpaper, which the museum had recently recreated from scraps dating back to Austen's day. The dining room looked particularly striking in arsenic green with a leaf motif.[32] This room is the holy of holies, for it contains Austen's writing table. The table was not what I had expected. The walnut top is less than half a metre in diameter and is supported by a single tripod column. It resembles a lamp stand, or an occasional table; its domesticity rather absurdly contradicts the heft of her novels. Still, it produces a profound reaction in those who pass through here. Many visitors choke, cry or hold their breath, or simply stand and stare.

Lovers of literature tend to fetishize the desks of famous writers, as if expecting the desk to retain some of the writer's energy or the power of their prose. To the writer, the desk may have been just something to lean on. The English professor Nicola Watson, who specializes in the cultural afterlives of authors and their texts, has pointed out that Austen's table is unusual among curated writers' desks in its want of distinguishing features: 'There is no claim to provenance, and few traces of "work". No paper, no ink, no sand-sifter, no proofs, no personal belongings, no books, no candle, no brass plaque or inscription.'[33] The table lacks a crucial component: her mahogany writing box, on which she would have rested her paper – it is on display at the British Library. Unadorned and empty, the table is nonetheless tremendously evocative. It allows us to insert Austen there and to conjure up the writer at work. *This* is where it happened. Constance Hill, who visited with her sister in 1901 when the house was being used as a working men's club, mused about sitting 'in the very room where Miss Jane Austen used to write'; they held the writing box in their hands and 'looked upon the firm, delicate handwriting of its owner'.[34]

We left Austen's desk and walked up the creaky staircase and into the bedroom that she shared with her sister Cassandra. I'm always tempted in places like these to be overly interactive with the surroundings, to touch all the things you're not supposed to. It was a struggle not to fling myself onto the four-poster bed. I sensed that Sophie and Abbie felt something similar as they rhapsodised over the clothes hanging in the bedroom. 'That is absolutely gorgeous, though quite small,' exclaimed Abbie as she contemplated the blue long-sleeved linen dress worn by Anne Hathaway in the biopic *Becoming Jane*. 'I'd like to make sleeves like that.' (She since has.)

A woman entered the room and, seeing Sophie and Abbie in their finery, asked them if they were part of the show. They giggled, not in the least offended. It led to a discussion about how, by participating in Regency cosplay and identifying with *that* era, they were refuting the social expectations of this one. 'It gives us the confidence not to worry about what other people think or what society dictates,' Sophie said. 'It's much the same with Austen's heroines in her novels. They had the attitude and the spirit to say, "You can't tell me what I'm going to do. I'm going to do what I want."'

Before anyone else could try to turn my friends into an exhibit, we scuttled down the corridor and into the room where some of Austen's most revered possessions were on display. Her embroidered muslin shawl was there, which Abbie was planning to replicate at home. 'I have the muslin and I have the thread!' We scrutinized two beautiful topaz crosses given to Austen and her sister by their younger brother Charles; a huge patchwork quilt that the sisters and their mother stitched together out of dress and furnishing fabrics; and a turquoise glass and ivory bead bracelet, a family heirloom that may have been worn by Jane.

Finally, we stopped before Austen's ring. In the hierarchy of deified objects, this ring is on a par with her writing table, for its provenance makes it certain that she wore it. It was made for delicate fingers: an unblemished turquoise stone set in a simple gold band. You can buy an exact replica in the museum's shop;

many Janeites, Sophie included, wear one as a keepsake or talisman. Sophie's was an eighteenth-birthday present from her mother and is one of her favourite possessions. She wears it every day. 'It's my bit of Jane that I have with me all the time,' she said.

———

In 2012, the year before the museum acquired the ring, it was sold at auction by Jane Austen's family to the American singer Kelly Clarkson, who collects Austen memorabilia. The British government quickly slapped an export ban on the piece, which allowed the museum to launch an appeal to buy it back. Clarkson had paid £152,450, which would have been excessive for most gold rings, but not for this one. Objects with extraordinary provenance have always commanded extraordinary prices, and there are usually plenty of collector-fans willing to raise their hand.

In recent years, fans have paid handsomely for basketball superstar Michael Jordan's Nike trainers ($560,000), Michael Jackson's velvet jacket ($65,625), Darth Vader's helmet from *Star Wars: The Empire Strikes Back* ($898,420), an early James Bond Aston Martin DB5 ($4.1 million), Emilia Earhart's leather flying cap ($825,000), a tennis racket smashed by Serena Williams during her 2018 defeat in the US Open ($20,910), the red dress worn by Kate Winslet in *Titanic* ($330,000), an armband discarded by Cristiano Ronaldo (€64,000), Elvis Presley's Bible (£59,000), Ringo Starr's drum kit ($2.2 million), John F. Kennedy's rocking chair ($453,500), Marilyn Monroe's chest X-rays ($45,000) and John Wayne's toupee ($6,250).

Many of these objects are aesthetically appealing, but this is not what makes them desirable – a brush with fame is what's required. Auctioneers have also managed to sell, without any difficulty, one of Lady Gaga's acrylic nails ($12,000), a kidney stone passed by William Shatner ($25,000), Britney Spears' positive pregnancy test ($5,000), Truman Capote's ashes ($43,750), one of John Lennon's molars ($31,200) and a piece of French toast half-eaten by Justin Timberlake ($1,025).

The silly prices that people are prepared to pay for celebrity relics bear no relation to their material value. The replica of Jane Austen's turquoise and gold ring costs £450. Presumably Kelly Clarkson thought that a mark-up of 33,800 per cent was reasonable for something that had sat on the author's finger. You might ask why she thought so. How can an object's perceived value be so much greater than its material one? What exactly is it that fans are paying for?

In many cultures, it is commonly believed that a person's essence can pass into their possessions through physical contact. The objects become psychologically contagious. The most contagious objects are physical remains. In Victorian times, it was traditional to keep hair from a deceased loved one (I have some from my great-great-grandmother). A lock of Jane Austen's hair is one of the Austen museum's most treasured possessions, though it is not always on display. Owning someone's hair gives you a special connection: the ability to actually touch them. Handwritten letters have a similar power. Something of the person is captured in the writing, or in the ink, or in the paper that they pressed on. In my youth, I used to collect the drumsticks of famous drummers; the sticks bore the scars of their playing, and seemed to possess something of their energy.

The Yale psychologists George Newman and Paul Bloom have

studied psychological contagion in both real-world settings and lab-based experiments. In 2014, they analysed data from the estate auctions of three high-profile individuals: John F. Kennedy, Jacqueline Onassis and Marilyn Monroe. They discovered that items that were perceived as having had greater contact with their owner, such as JFK's sweater or Marilyn's necklace, generally attracted higher bids than more anonymous items such as furniture, regardless of their material value. To explore this further, they conducted a separate experiment in which they tested people's willingness to pay for a celebrity's sweater that had been sterilized, with all residue of the previous owner removed. The sterilized sweater proved far less appealing: removing the 'essence' of the celebrity significantly reduced its value.[35]

Their findings convinced Newman and Bloom that a belief in psychological contagion is pervasive in contemporary Western societies. We all want our heroes to live for ever, and this is a way of granting them immortality. Jane Austen's body will not be rising up any day soon from beneath the floor of Winchester Cathedral, but at least we can feel connected to her through her ring.

———

As we walked back down the creaky staircase, Sophie and Abbie pondered on what Jane Austen would be like were she alive today. 'I'd have so many questions to ask her,' said Sophie. Abbie wondered if she'd be on Twitter. Almost certainly, she decided. 'I don't think she'd care what people said. She'd be open with her opinions and you'd just either love it or not. I think she'd own up to her mistakes. Her humility comes across in her books and her characters.' They both decided that she would be a lot of fun, and they'd definitely want to be her friend. They already are, I suggested. 'That's what it feels like!' exclaimed Sophie. This conversation being likely to run into the afternoon, we left Jane's house and headed to the Cassandra's Cup cafe across the road for – what else? – a reviving cup of tea.

6

Animal Minds

NOT LONG AGO, I had a conversation with a bear.

The bear was in reality a man, a man who feels in his bones that he is a bear. In the academic vernacular, he is a therian: someone who believes from a young age that they are an animal trapped inside a human body, a state of being known as therianthropy.[1] If you've never heard of therians, that's hardly surprising: there are not many of them,[2] and they have rarely been the subject of academic study.

The dysphoria that comes from believing that you were born in the wrong species is so far from the regular human experience that therians struggle to describe it. Ask them what it is like to be an animal and they will ask you, quite reasonably, if you can describe what it is like to be a human. They know what they know, and it is not what you know.

Therianthropy is no passing fancy. It is not an obsession or a mental disorder. It is a conviction, one that therians spend their entire lives trying to accommodate. They are not fans in the usual sense; their passion chooses them. They are included here as an example of a social group on the fringes of society that has a

117

big influence on the well-being of its members. The therian community defines itself as a fandom and shares many of the psychological characteristics of regular fandoms. Therians are on a quest for identity, meaning and a sense of belonging just like Janeites, Trekkies and Potterheads. More than any other fandom, they illustrate the protective effects of being part of a group: their life experience and their psychology are so different to most people's that they often feel profoundly isolated until they find each other. This chapter describes what it is like on an individual level to identify as another species, and how therians work together as a community to resolve this incongruity. In their struggle to be animal, therians can teach the rest of us a lot about what it is to be human.

———

My friend the bear, who goes by the sobriquet BearX,[3] lives an improbably normal life. He is married. He has two children. His career in engineering has afforded him a nice house and a comfortable middle-class life. As he says, 'If you didn't know something was up, you wouldn't know anything was up.' He has many bearish qualities: he is friendly, jovial, broad-chested, huggable. The arc of his existence is best summed up by the biographical tagline he uses in online forums: 'Grew up in the country. Was supposed to be a bear. Wasn't.'

I first learned about therianthropy while talking to Kathy Gerbasi, a social psychologist who specializes in relationships between humans and animals. Gerbasi learned about therians while studying furries, the fans of anthropomorphic animal characters that we encountered in Chapter 3. One year at a furry convention, she conducted a survey that included the following two questions: 'Do you consider yourself to be less than 100 per cent human?', and 'If you could be 0 per cent human, would you be?' Furries feel an affinity with animals, but that's generally as far as it goes. So when a few of her respondents answered yes to both questions, she knew that she was dealing with people who were fundamentally atypical.

Since then, Gerbasi has held several discussion groups with therians, who she describes as 'very sincere'. 'They look like people,' she says. 'They mostly behave like people. They hold jobs. They have relationships. But they feel they're playing at being human. When they're interacting with the public, behaving the way they're supposed to, they feel they're not being true to themselves. If you really talk to them, they'll tell you that deep inside they are not a person.'

When psychologists investigate an unusual pattern of behaviour, they look for common attributes that may help explain it such as age, gender, race, class, culture, geography or socio-economic status. So far, Gerbasi and the handful of other psychologists who have studied therians have failed to find any. They seem to be a diverse bunch. I've talked to therians in their teens and in their seventies, of female, male and undetermined gender, living in the Netherlands, the US, Canada, Slovenia, the UK, France, Norway, Germany, Belgium and Serbia. Nothing in their demographics or their backgrounds predicts their shared fate.

The only thing that can be said with certainty about almost all therians is that they recognize early on – often when they are as young as six – that they are different in body and spirit from those around them. They feel 'off', separated from humanity, and this estrangement defines the rest of their lives.

In what way 'off'?

'I had an internal sense as a kid that I was supposed to be bigger, heavier and sort of stand up tall,' says BearX. 'Later, I worked out that bears fit everything that I felt. It led me to think that maybe I was supposed to have been born a bear and there was some kind of cataclysmic failure in the universe's sorting system. Some nights I would break down crying and begging God, "Why am I like this and can you fix it?" After a while, I realized God wasn't going to fix it.'

Caesar, a communications technician in his mid-thirties who identifies as a coyote, remembers feeling 'odd' and 'distant to people' in his second year at primary school. By the time he reached his teens, he had the feeling that he was significantly out of the ordinary without understanding why. 'I remember feeling very animal. Maybe the best way to put it is that humans think with their emotions or on a higher level of cognition, but the way I responded to a situation was more instinctual, not calculating.'

As they grow up, therians move from having a general sense of feeling not quite human to a more concrete awareness of the kind of animal they are. Eventually, they will land on the particular species that feels right, their 'theriotype'. The most common theriotypes are predator species such as wolves and large cats. As with furries, culture plays a role: jaguars are more common in South America, and foxes in Japan, whose folklore contains many stories of people being possessed by a fox.[4] Almost all therians are mammals. While researching this chapter, I talked to six wolves, two snow leopards, two brown bears, two coyotes, a bonobo, a striped hyena, a dolphin and a pine marten. One of the wolves lived in a house with a bear, a coyote, a badger and some sort of reptile. I also talked to three werewolves and a couple of dragons. Mythical or fantasy creatures are no less valid, though their owners are differentiated in the community as 'otherkin'.

———

A peculiar and often alarming characteristic of being a therian – one that both distinguishes and unites them as a group – is the feeling that you have phantom body parts. All the therians I met were reconciled to the reality that they were living in a fully human body and that, sadly, this would always be the case. But for some of them, this is a difficult reality to accept when their brain is telling them otherwise.[5]

Blayz, a wolf–dog hybrid, lives with the permanent sensation of a prominent muzzle, fangs and a long canine tongue, and a tail that wags or droops on command. 'Going around corners, I will alter the movement of my frame to keep my tail from getting caught in doors or swiping cups off the table,' he says. Another wolf, a young woman in the American north-west who goes by the name Little Wolf, feels like she has a 'constant tail where there obviously is none' and experiences the frequent urge to walk on her toes. Caesar, the coyote, is often convinced he has outsized ears that he can manipulate like antennae. Both my bear interviewees complained about having hands that feel completely different to how they look. BearX fantasizes about one day acquiring a virtual reality device that would allow him to look down and see paws instead of hands and feet.

I spoke with a snow leopard – an American woman in her early twenties – who has been saddled with the full range of phantom phenomena. 'No matter what, I always have a phantom tail,' she explained. 'Even as a kid, I remember feeling like I had a tail and telling people it was invisible. It's as much a part of me as my arms and legs, really. I also have constant phantom paws and a muzzle, which can make eating and drinking funny sometimes. I'm likely to miss my mouth if I'm not thinking about it, because I feel like my mouth is a little farther out like a snout than like human lips. Besides that, I often get feelings of leopard ears on my head, whiskers, fur and an array of other animal-like features.'

To feel body parts where none could possibly have existed is not as biologically improbable as it sounds. Studies of amputees and of people born with missing arms and legs have shown that it is not necessary to have a physical body to experience one, and that limbs that have always been absent can still be represented in the sensory and motor regions of the brain. Perception of the body as a single unit is generated almost entirely by the brain's neural networks; sensory information plays only a minor role. The psychologist Ronald Melzack, an expert on phantom pain, proposed that the brain continuously generates a pattern of impulses that indicate that the body is intact and 'unequivocally one's own', even if it isn't. This pattern, which Melzack called a 'neurosignature', is genetically determined and characteristic of each individual.[6] It is not inconceivable that someone born with an atypical neurosignature might experience a body that is out of kilter with the one they possess. So far, no one has systematically examined the brains of therians to see if their neural patterns reflect what they feel.

Therians who are acclimatized to their animal side often find their phantom experiences reassuring or even pleasurable, since they confirm for them the existence of an identity that they have been trying hard to accept. Phantom body parts can make you feel more animal, but it can be a let-down when you recognize that you don't have the superpowers you thought you did. When Caesar realizes yet again that he cannot direct his ears to hone in on a distant sound, he has the sobering thought that what he is trying to do is 'in direct conflict with my own biology'. He regrets very much that he does not have fur. 'I generally feel very naked and exposed, like a shaved dog.'

Kathy Gerbasi, in one of her studies, interviewed a therian who felt that they were a creature with wings. When she asked them what it was like when their 'wings' were fully out, they told her it made them frustrated because they knew they couldn't fly. Therians are frequently dissatisfied that they cannot do the things their phantom bodies tell them they should. Many of them avoid looking in mirrors because it reminds them that they are not what they think they are. The cognitive dissonance can be overwhelming.

———

Phantom body parts are not the only manifestation of therians' dissociative reality. Many of them report having 'perception shifts': altered states of consciousness in which they transition to a mindset more characteristic of an animal. Almost all my interviewees, regardless of species, described their behaviour during these episodes as 'instinctive', 'focused' and 'aware', their cognition as 'suspended', their thoughts devoid of words. One of the most common perception shifts, particularly among canine therians, is an imperative to walk or run on four limbs. 'Having the sensation of being able to move around on all fours is almost indescribable,' says wolf–dog Blayz. 'It's a humbling experience that makes me feel close to all of nature. Every move I make seems fluid. I feel intimately connected to my environment, like my body is just an eyeball and the rest of creation is my actual body. Tough to describe!'

Therians commonly resort to figurative language to explain their condition. Their experience is so otherworldly that they must approach it obliquely in order to understand. Blayz's 'awakening' – the point at which he realized why he felt so strange – came when he was sixteen while watching *Balto*, an animated film about a wolf–dog who leads a sled team across hundreds of miles of frozen wilderness to rescue a group of children. Blayz remembers his 'enormous empathic reaction' to the hero and the story. Popular culture, rich in imagery and metaphor, is often where young people start their search for meaning; it's no different for therians.

Perception shifts and phantom limbs may be disconcerting, but they can be useful in helping therians to settle on their theriotype. If you feel claws for hands, you're probably a bear; if you have the urge to chase deer, you're probably a wolf. If you feel a desire while standing in a crowd to bite into the spine of the person in front of you, as one therian acknowledged in a recent study, then you may be an African lioness, one of the few remaining predators of humans.[7] Recognition can bring a sense of resolution. Blayz says that while the path to understanding that he was a wolf–dog was 'painful, lonely and frustrating', once he had accepted it he felt better about who he was. Since then, he says, 'I have always been happy and proud of the inner fur I wear!'

Finding your theriotype can be a struggle. Most therians make their decision only after a great deal of research and thought.

The community encourages its members to be scientifically rigorous: outlandish claims that would give ammunition to sceptics, such as the idea that it's possible to physically transform into an animal, are dismissed as 'fluff'. On therian forums, moderators frequently rebuke contributors for promoting theories that would break the laws of physics, and they are quick to correct errors in their morphological or behavioural descriptions of species, such as the suggestion that wolves have red eyes, or that all canines hunt in packs.

The basic proposition that therians face is simple: I'm human and I feel like an animal, which animal am I? Resolving this problem is fraught and complex. Alliana, who has felt 'off' since the age of eight, decided that she must be werewolf on account of her anger-driven perception shifts ('I feel like there's a raging beast inside me'). She then followed up on this intuition by digging into the literature. 'The more I researched them, the more it became apparent that I was one.' In her journey, she has never felt that she had a choice. 'If I had a choice, I would rather not have a theriotype at all and just be comfortable in my own skin.'

For therians, 'finding yourself' – that nebulous ideal promoted by the self-help industry – is obligatory. Although discovery may bring relief, it does not help with the bigger questions: Why am I this way? Where did I come from? What is the meaning of my existence? Therians spend a lot of time pondering them. Science doesn't provide many answers, so they can only speculate. Therianthropy may be a developmental response to early trauma or a childhood fixation on animals, or it may be a result of abnormal brain wiring. People of a spiritual inclination might think of it in terms of reincarnation or a 'misplaced soul'. There's no way of knowing. Gerbasi has found that therians long for an explanation. 'They want to understand why they are the way they are.' All she can tell them is that their brains work a little differently to most people's.

———

Some psychologists believe that the distress suffered by therians is similar to the distress suffered by people whose sex at birth does not match the way they feel. The comparison is often made by therians themselves, a minority of whom are transgender as well as 'transspecies' (as they sometimes put it). Not all transgender people are comfortable with this analogy, fearing that it complicates the public discourse and undermines their movement's drive for recognition. The obvious parallel between the two groups is their all-consuming experience of dysmorphia, the perception that your body is wrong; the obvious difference is that while you can change your gender, you cannot do anything about your species.

In psychiatry, therianthropy is generally viewed as a mental disorder, or a symptom of psychosis or schizophrenia. It is erroneously considered to be synonymous with clinical lycanthropy, a condition related to schizophrenia that was first described in 1988.[8] The definition of clinical lycanthropy is based on observations of twelve patients at McLean Hospital in Boston whose delusions and hallucinations convinced them that they had transformed into an animal. Sufferers appear to have trouble distinguishing between their own bodily sensations and external phenomena, possibly because of an abnormality in the way their brain cells communicate. In her book *Unthinkable: An Extraordinary Journey through the World's Strangest Brains*, Helen Thomson describes meeting a lycanthrope who periodically becomes convinced that he has turned into a tiger; her interview with him had to be cut short when he suddenly started growling and threatening to attack her, a relapse his doctors blamed on his failure to take his anti-psychotic medication.[9]

Therians rarely report any of the clinical symptoms of lycanthropy. They are not delusional or psychotic. Their animalistic feelings are a perpetual feature of their state of being and are not alleviated by medication. They are aware, often to their profound disappointment, that they can never transform into animals. The medical profession's impulse to diagnose them has less to do with clinical evidence than the age-old tendency to pathologize behaviours and conditions that challenge social norms. The most we can say about the medical status of therians is that they are neurological outliers – hardly a signal of illness.

In 2019 Helen Clegg, a psychologist at the University of Buckingham, led the first comprehensive investigation into the well-being and mental health of therians. She recruited one hundred and twelve across a broad range of ages, genders, ethnicities and species. Among them were wolves, foxes, dogs, coyotes, big cats, domestic cats, cougars, dragons, birds, a jackal, a dingo, a deer, a racoon, a snake, a shark and a couple of dinosaurs. Clegg's team found that a disproportionate number of them had been diagnosed with autism (7.69 per cent compared with 1.5 per cent in the general US population), though it is not clear how the two conditions are linked. They also found that, compared with a control group, many therians struggle with relationships and social skills. This could be due to cognitive factors, or it could be because social taboos around

therianthropy make it difficult for them to reveal this fundamental aspect of themselves to anyone else. When you are
forced to hide your true nature, communicating with others
can be a challenge.[10]

Social difficulties aside, the therians in Clegg's study scored
just as highly as non-therians on several standard measures of
psychological well-being, including personal growth, purpose in
life and self-acceptance. They scored *higher* than non-therians on
the psychological measure for autonomy – the degree to which
you instigate and take responsibility for your own behaviour. The
researchers concluded: 'The findings suggest that therians are
functioning well.'

Their study also noted that many of the therians displayed
'schizotypal' personality traits, such as a tendency to have
unusual perceptual and other cognitive experiences. In the
general population, these traits are associated with psychosis and
schizophrenia, but these therians mostly found their experiences
enriching rather than distressing. Clegg suggests that this is
because they have found a way to integrate their fantastical
thoughts and beliefs into a coherent narrative that allows them
to make sense of the way they feel. This would explain why
therians are at such pains to understand their therianthropy and
to work out which species they are – and why, once 'awakened',
they sleep more easily.[11]

Therianthropy may not be a mental illness, but this does not
change the reality that it can be very hard to live with. One
summer afternoon, I spoke via video link to Azi, a Mexican wolf
living in Tennessee who has perception shifts around thirty times
a day. Therian friends of his told me that his experience is more
extreme than anyone they know – for much of the time, he is

more wolf than human. During our initial correspondence he was apprehensive, fearing negative publicity, but when we finally spoke he was open, eloquent and precise. He wore a khaki base-ball cap and a T-shirt depicting a wolf family, which reflected his role as an advocate and fundraiser for the conservation of Mexican grey wolves. He is fighting to preserve an endangered species – of which he himself is one. He thinks his therianthropy is due to reincarnation, believing that he has the soul of a wolf that was poached in New Mexico in the 1950s or 1960s.

Azi calls his perceptual changes between human and wolf 'snap shifts', because they arrive suddenly and can pass just as quickly. When they happen, he says, 'the human part of me is turned off. Mentally, I'm gone. The wolf mindset is running this body. I'm in the passenger seat and the wolf is doing whatever he wants to, and I'm thinking, "When this is over, I'll go and do so and so." It's very dissociative.' His shifts are hard to suppress, and hard to control when they are on. He often finds himself growling, snarling, down on all fours, walking on his toes or, if the oppor-tunity presents itself, chasing deer. It can be physically exhausting. He says it is like being deeply engaged in a movie. Afterwards he can remember everything, but at the time he is not the one running the show. 'My human side is pushed all the way down. It's very surreal.'

Admitting to yourself that you are a wolf – or a bear, badger, beaver or anything else – can bring comfort, because it gives you an identity, a representation of who you are that you can relate to. It is not unlike the ostracized Harry Potter fan in Chapter 3 who found a new understanding of herself among the misfits and eccentrics of Hogwarts. But for therians this recognition is often bittersweet. Elizabeth Fein, a clinical psychologist who has worked closely with Kathy Gerbasi, says acceptance of therian-thropy can bring sadness or a sense of estrangement. 'It's like, "I'm always going to be different, I'm always going to be kind of separate from humanity. I'm never going to have the right body. There's always going to be this thing about me that will never be right."'[12] BearX told me that the realization that he was a bear 'was accompanied by this terrible sense of grief about my own humanity'. He'd found one identity and lost another.

Azi vividly remembers the moment in his early thirties when he acknowledged the wolf within. It was 4.45 p.m. on 3 May 2015, he was standing 'in an open field next to a pond' talking to a friend when he suddenly decided to stop running from who he was. 'It felt like a weight was lifted from me. I felt happy like never before.' The feeling didn't last. Azi had spent most of his life suppressing his animal feelings, 'fearful of what was inside me, which didn't line up with what we as humans expect to feel'. Surrendering to it brought him some relief, but the fear that it could consume him has never really left (he is not the only therian who feels this way). 'I've come a long way, and my fears aren't nearly as strong as they used to be. But I'm sure I will never fully overcome them.'

Towards the end of my video call with Azi, my cat Cecil jumped up onto my laptop and started nuzzling the screen, hoping for some attention. I noticed that Azi looked away and appeared to disengage for a moment. When I asked him about this, he admitted that as a wolf, few things are more inflammatory than being stared at by a cat. 'The wolf doesn't like them and wants to give chase', he explained, a feeling he managed to suppress on this occasion. He has to contend with provocations like this whenever he goes out in public – a loud noise, a fleeing animal, a bothersome human – and he must always be on his guard to stop himself shifting to wolf.

Therianthropy presents its adherents with not so much a psychological challenge as an existential one. Knowing that they are an animal, they must ask themselves how they should live as a human. Therians harmonize their dual identities in all kinds of creative ways. Lopori, a bonobo who lives in the UK, spends as much time as possible at his local zoo, where he watches the apes and interacts with them through the glass. 'Being in the company of apes makes me calm and joyful,' he says. 'The longer I spend away from that zoo, the more fragile my emotional state is; the more I get to visit, the more resilient and content I am.' Azi snuggles up with his wolf pup soft toy: 'It helps control the wolf and calm it down; it seems to think the pup is real'. Caesar wears his artificial coyote paws and tail to bed. 'I like waking up and seeing my paws.' BearX goes into the woods whenever he can. Some wolves get together for communal 'howls' – camping trips for therians.

For therians who are also Christian, there is the additional question of whether their religion is compatible with their therianthropy – can you be redeemed if you are a soul in the wrong body or believe you had past lives? Most of them resolve this by thinking that there must be a reason why they feel the way they do. 'I don't have the answer yet,' says the snow leopard with the phantom limbs. 'As long as I am not hurting anyone or myself, I try to not let those questions bug me too much.' Why should she fret? After all, religion is a long journey in search of an elusive truth – therians have been on that road most of their lives.

———

Prince Hanzoku being terrorized by a shape-shifting fox,
by Utagawa Kuniyoshi, 1798–1861. (Wikimedia Commons)

The scale of the challenge that therians face in trying to reconcile their human bodies with their animal minds – and in convincing non-therians to take them seriously – may be partly a function of the culture they live in. In the West, for much of the past two millennia we have considered ourselves distinct from the rest of the animal kingdom, elevated by cognition, intelligence, language, morality and culture. In the first chapter of the book of Genesis, God granted humans 'dominion over the fish of the sea, over the birds of the air, and over every living thing that moves on the earth',[13] and the Judaeo-Christian tradition wasted no time in making that creation story gospel. Philosophers from Aristotle to Kant have emphasized our superiority over nature, reasoning that animals, lacking souls or anything approaching the human mind, are simply – as Descartes put it – mindless automata or brutes.[14] Human exceptionalism has led to the reckless exploitation of the planet and a narrow attitude towards the moral status of animals. But this is almost exclusively a Western view, and if you look back over the tens of thousands of years of human existence, you'll realize that it is a very recent one. The line separating human and other has not always been so well defined.

Many cultures recognize animals as either deities or ancestors. A popular Tibetan creation myth maintains that Tibetans are descended from a meditating monkey, while in Turkic mythology all Turkic peoples originate from a she-wolf named Asena. Many indigenous groups have an animistic perspective, believing that animals, plants, rivers, rocks and other natural features have a spiritual essence, just as humans do. Ancient Egyptians considered certain animals sacred; they treated cats with great reverence and mourned and mummified them on their death. Today, plenty of cat owners think of their pets as possessing an intuition far beyond the human. Treating a pet like a person is acceptable even in the Anthropocene.[15]

In certain cases, the divide between species has been conspicuously absent. Some of the earliest pieces of art depict human–animal hybrids. Famous examples include the Lion Man, a 35,000-year-old lion-headed figurine carved from the tusk of a mammoth, which was found in Hohlenstein-Stadel, a cave in southern Germany, and the Sorcerer, a 15,000-year-old cave painting in south-western France that resembles a humanoid stag. It is hard to know what they mean, though their existence is suggestive of a worldview quite different to the modern anthropocentric one. They may represent a shaman's attempt to communicate with an animal, to transform into one or to tap into its physical or spiritual qualities.

Stories about people who 'shape-shift' between human and animal form have persisted throughout recorded history. The Epic of Gilgamesh, written around 4,000 years ago, describes the friendship between a king and a primitive wild man – thought to be a version of the bull-man that frequently appears in ancient Mesopotamian art – who lives like an animal until he is seduced and tamed by a prostitute. Ancient Egyptians believed that certain deities were capable of switching from human to animal as it suited them. Ubiquitous in Japanese mythology are *kitsune*, mischievous foxes with multiple tails and magical powers that can also take human form. Among the Navajo people in the American south-west, some of the greatest evils are thought to be the work of skin-walkers, shamans who have the power to turn into coyotes, foxes, wolves, owls or crows. In Mexico and central America there exist magicians or clairvoyants called *naguales* who while under the influence of a potent intoxicant can transform themselves into a jaguar, donkey, bat, dog, weasel or owl; the sixteenth-century missionary Joseph de Acosta noted that these sorcerers can 'take any shape they choose, and fly through the air with wonderful rapidity and for long distances'.[16]

European folklore has its own constellation of shape-shifting heroes and villains. The Viking warriors known as berserkers dressed for battle in the skins of bears and wolves, which they believed gave them the animals' strength and ferocity. Medieval witches were persecuted by the Church for their habit of trans-forming into cats, owls, ravens and rabbits. The most notorious shape-shifter is the werewolf, a human who metamorphoses into a cannibalistic wolf at full moon. Many of these creatures live on in the popular imagination. Derivations of them appear regularly in novels and films – the *Harry Potter* and *Game of Thrones* series are carnivals of shape-shifting – and occasionally in news reports: since 1975, a werewolf has been 'sighted' a couple of dozen times in the woods and cemeteries of Cannock Chase in central England, scaring the wits out of locals before rearing up and escaping on its two hind legs.[17]

What might induce someone to transform into an animal? They may long for some quality denied to humans, such as the speed of a cheetah, the endurance of a stag or the cunning of a fox. They may wish to learn an animal's habits in order to hunt it more effectively, or simply to be free of the responsibilities of being human. When you think about it, who wouldn't want to give it a go?

A few years ago Thomas Thwaites, a British artist and designer, devised an experiment to find out what it would be like to live as a goat. He arranged for an engineer to make him some prosthetic limbs that would allow him to gallop downhill, consulted animal behaviourists for an insight into goat psychology, and even considered a fecal transplant that would help him digest grass (this was rejected on health grounds). He then spent three days grazing on all fours with a herd of goats on a Swiss mountain. He mostly had a pleasant time; the farmer who owned the goats reckoned that Thwaites had been accepted by the herd, even though he had trouble keeping up with them.

What did he learn from the experience? In his book *Goat Man: How I Took a Holiday from Being Human*, Thwaites writes that goat life involves 'walking to a patch of grass and eating it for five minutes or so. Walking to another patch of grass, eating that. And so on and so forth.'[18] Still, he learned about the nutritional qualities of different types of grass, and how difficult it is for bipeds to walk downhill on all fours. Later, he reflected on the ways the experience had changed his perspective, and how living like an animal could release us from the confabulatory narratives that we build around our lives and that cause us endless worry:

> It's important to remember every now and again that we are animals, because it helps us to think ourselves away from some of the more crazy aspects of our society and humanity. Being an animal would help us remember that there is no manifest destiny to the human species – we are just among all these other creatures.[19]

––––––

A world in which animals were treated as human and humans were treated as animals would be a lot easier for therians to live in. One of the most difficult things about being a therian is the fear of public ridicule, which forces them to hide who they really are. 'Our lives would be immeasurably improved if people accepted it, if it wasn't considered strange,' BearX told me. 'That feeling of being accepted – that's what everybody wants.' It's hard to live with a condition that the rest of society disavows. Without validation, you have little access to social support. The same principle explains why military personnel fighting in unpopular campaigns are at higher risk of trauma-related illness when they return home.[20] Public condemnation is social alienation, a corrosive punishment.[21]

Many of the therians I spoke to have not told their families or close friends about their therianthropy. 'Ha, you kidding?' replies Copycat, a teenage coyote, when I ask him if he has opened up about his condition. 'When I tried sharing my therian side to my family, they made fun of it. I typically don't tell anyone about it unless I know they'll be chill.' Kathy Gerbasi, the psychologist who studies therians, explains that self-disclosure can be perilous. 'Inside yourself you can say, "I'm really not like other people, I'm really a fox." But wait a minute, that's another problem: "Who can I tell that I'm really a fox?"' Feeling like an animal, living like a human, unable to commit to either, therians are caught in a shadowland, suspended between two worlds.

Thankfully, they have each other. The modern therian community came into being in 1993 on the message boards of an online werewolf fan group called alt.horror.werewolves. It has since evolved into a vibrant network of moderated communities, discussion forums, advice boards and other resources, with thousands of active participants and enduring friendships. BearX, who helped set up the first therian online group in 1993, says they support each other in many different ways – socially, financially, emotionally. 'You develop astonishingly close friendships, because you have this unusual shared experience,' he says.

I heard similar versions of this story over and over from different therians. Caesar the coyote told me that his introduction to the community was 'unquestionably one of the happiest moments of my life: finding out that you're not alone, that these feelings and experiences do have some validity beyond myself, that I'm not necessarily on a deserted island after all'. Blayz, who spent years trying to figure out his strange canine sensations, came close to dismissing them as 'the delusions of a madman, nothing more than a side-effect of mental illness'. When he discovered that he wasn't the only one who felt this way, 'it was like an enormous avalanche of "aha" moments all at once. So many of my own experiences and conclusions were echoed by this group of real people out there in the world. It was overwhelming! It felt like salvation. Finding out about other therians may have saved both my sanity and my life.'

As with any social group, the therian community entertains plenty of drama; therians disagree with each other like anyone else. There are differences of opinion, for example, over the causes of therianthropy, the distinction between therians and otherkin, and whether it is appropriate to discuss the sexual feelings that some therians have towards animals.[22] But the prevailing impression is that the community is a source of great strength, and that many therians would be lost without their therian family. In this way, it resembles other fandoms. Social psychologists have found that members of minority or disadvantaged groups who experience persistent prejudice or criticism respond by identifying more closely with their own group, offsetting any potential harm with the psychological advantages of belonging. It might sound paradoxical, but stigma can become a strength when shared with others.[23]

'Therians are really weird,' one of the coyotes says to me in a moment of exasperation. But perhaps it's a matter of perspective. In certain cultures, and in certain eras, they have been regarded as less weird; among other therians, their behaviour is completely normal. Most therians want to be accepted by the wider world, though it's reassuring for them to know that they will always be accepted by their own. Life looks different when you're part of a pack. It doesn't matter whether you're a bear, a wolf, a coyote, a leopard, a hyena, a dinosaur or an owl. If you're animal, you're in.

The life-long struggle that therians must endure is eased by their membership of a sympathetic community. You don't need to be part of a collective to enjoy being a fan, but it can help. As we'll see in the next chapter, harbouring a fannish passion can be a trial, particularly when it rubs up against popular opinion. In such cases, fans need all the support they can get.

7

Through the Bad Times and the Good

THE INTERNET MOVIE DATABASE lists 147 movies about obsessed fans.[1] Quite a few of them have the title 'The Fan', or variations thereof. My favourite of these is *Der Fan*, a German production from 1982 about a teenage girl who is obsessed with a pop singer. It begins predictably enough – she writes him dozens of letters – but the ending is harder to foresee. When he fails to reply, she intercepts him outside one of his gigs, hangs out in his dressing room, has sex with him, bludgeons him to death with a statue, has sex with him again, cuts up his body, grinds up his bones – except for one of his feet which she marinades, roasts and eats – then cleans up his blood with her tongue. It's a satisfying ninety-two minutes.

Films like *Der Fan* tap into a stereotype that fans have had to endure since the emergence of popular culture (the word is still associated with 'fanatic' in the public consciousness). Characterized as geeks, misfits, mindless consumers, hysterics, fantasists and psychopaths, they are feared either as obsessive loners who spend their lives fretting in their bedrooms (like the protagonist in most fan movies) or as members of a frenzied mob (screaming girls at a One Direction concert). They are considered weird when they do fannish things on their own and weird when they do them together.

'The thin line between love and hate, between free will and fate, gradually disappears for the fan in the attic, lumping around his unacknowledged, unwanted love like an embarrassing erection,' noted Julie Burchill in *Damaged Gods*, her 1986 critique of celebrity culture. 'And the love turns into a weapon as he realizes he can never touch the one he wants, except with a bullet.'[2] The usual case study for this kind of depiction of fannish obsession is Mark Chapman, John Lennon's killer, though he is a poor model since he suffered from a major personality disorder.[3] Even Scotland Yard has entertained the idea that engaging with popular culture could turn sane people into murderers. In the months leading up to the Millennium, it prepared itself for the possibility of an 'act of extreme violence' such as a mass cult suicide inspired by popular science-fiction shows like *Star Trek* and *The X-Files*. According to an internal memo, it was concerned about 'the devotion certain groups and individuals ascribe to the contents of these programmes', warning that the makers knew exactly 'what psychological buttons to press'.[4]

'Mad fan', 'sad fan', 'obsessive fan'. These labels may be entirely inaccurate, but the stigma they carry affects all fans. Fearing ridicule or criticism, they have often been reluctant to 'out' themselves to people who do not share their enthusiasms. In a study of Kate Bush fans in 2002, Laura Vroomen at the University of Warwick found that nearly half her subjects declined to identify themselves as fans because they disliked the negative undertones, even though they were passionate about the singer and her music. 'The word "fan" has taken on rather sinister connotations recently

– people rifling through dustbins, *Misery* [a Stephen King book about an obsessive fan], being an anorak!' one of them told her. 'That's not me. [A fan is] primarily, someone who has an appreciation of an artist's work, and finds it interesting and/or joyful. But language is symbolic and changing, and maybe "fan" now means something more.'[5]

In *Starlust*, the anthology of 1980s fan testimonials collected by the cultural commentators Fred and Judy Vermorel, the sixteen-year-old Barry Manilow devotee called Helen who we encountered in Chapter 4 says she assumed she was 'some kind of lunatic' because no one else she knew loved her hero like she did. 'It's very, very difficult when you're the only person who believes in something with all your heart and other people say: "What?!" You start questioning yourself: Am I going round the twist? Am I basically insecure? Are my emotions all over the place? Is what I'm feeling right?' Only when she joined a local fan club did she realize for the first time that what she was feeling was normal.[6]

The shadow of the negative stereotype does not fall on all fans equally. Sports fans are rarely shamed for being excessively zealous – their commitment to the cause is expected, even applauded. As I write this, the men's Euro 2020 football championships (held in 2021 because of the pandemic) are nearing their finale, and every day the British newspapers publish stories about England fans who made extraordinary sacrifices amid Covid travel restrictions to watch their team play, or about fans who celebrated a win by stripping down to their St George's cross-themed underwear and throwing beer at their mates, or about others who dressed their dogs in England shirts and scarves to show their 'suppawt' for 'our boys', and all this is reported unflinchingly as if such behaviours were a rite of passage or part of a rich cultural heritage. Lynn Zubernis, a clinical psychologist who has been studying fans for nearly two decades, says sports fans – and particularly male sports fans – 'continue to get a pass across the board'.[7] In an interview a few years ago, she explained:

> The degree of ridicule that a male sports fan experiences – even if he paints himself half-green and half-white and goes to an Eagles game half-naked – is vastly different than the potential ridicule tossed at a male media fan who paints himself green and white and goes to Comic Con half-naked as an alien something-or-other.[8]

Sports is one of the few male-dominated fandoms, and it's possible that the shaming of pop culture fandoms, which tend to be female-dominated, is partly a response by some men to what they perceive to be inappropriate behaviour by women. Fortunately, in recent years it has become easier for fans of all kinds to show their colours without being humiliated for it. Zubernis suggests this is due to the proliferation of social media platforms such as Tumblr, Reddit, Facebook, Instagram and Twitter, each of which has its own norms and values that determine what is acceptable. 'The sheer heterogeneity has changed how fans relate to each other and to the broader culture,' she told me over email.[9] Fan communities have become part of the mainstream, making it easier than ever to participate in the conversation. This hasn't stopped fans disrespecting other fans, or being disrespected by non-fans. Social media can be vile. Misogyny is still a big problem. Remember Gamergate?

In case you missed it, Gamergate was a campaign of

harassment directed at women in the video-game industry by men who were unhappy at the growing female influence in what had been a predominantly male culture. It kicked off in 2013 after the developer Zoe Quinn released Depression Quest, a text-based game based on her own experience of the illness. For months afterwards, Quinn received death threats, rape threats and persistent online abuse from gamers who seemed irritated that she had subverted the traditional violence-based format. The abusers then targeted other women, including the feminist media critic Anita Sarkeesian, who was forced to flee her home after she criticized the trolls in a YouTube video. In an article for *Ars Technica*, the writer Casey Johnston remarked on the 'profound irony that one woman who dared point out some of the misogyny in video games was so deluged by misogynistic threats over how there is no misogyny in video games that she was driven into hiding'.[10] To this day, Gamergate rumbles on in Twitter threads and Reddit forums. Female gamers are still being attacked, and they continue to speak out while also creating and participating, even though their fandom is not a safe one.[11]

The toxicity that exists in online conversations about popular culture hasn't discouraged fans from taking part. Every major television drama series is shadowed by a lively discussion on social media about characters and plot, what might happen and what *should* happen, and where the producers have gone wrong. The final episode invariably triggers an outpouring of criticism from fans who had hoped for a different ending or a more convincing redemption for their favourite character. When the historical fantasy series *Game of Thrones* concluded in 2019 with Jon Snow, one of its most popular protagonists, killing his queen and lover Daenerys Targaryen (who was also, confusingly, his aunt), around two million people signed a petition demanding that the producers reshoot it. A similar reaction followed the release of the last *Star Wars* film *The Rise of Skywalker* – in fact, just about every *Star Wars* film that has ever been made. *Skywalker* was unpopular because the previous episode in the franchise, *The Last Jedi*, had hinted at the coming together of good (in the form of Rey, a feisty scavenger) and evil (the dark warrior Kylo Ren). This fan fantasy did eventually take place, only for Kylo Ren to die immediately after their first kiss.

A high degree of fan interaction is inevitable with film franchises and television series since they develop over time and draw their audiences into meandering narrative arcs (*Game of Thrones* lasted eight seasons; *Star Wars* has been going since 1977). At some level, these shows are collaborations between those who make them and those who watch. Most producers care greatly what fans think and use test screenings, trailers and media 'leaks' to gauge their reaction to future scenarios. Fans, being human, rarely agree on the critique of a show (many viewers loved the *Game of Thrones* finale); in trying to please them all, producers risk provoking and patronising them in equal measure.

Although *Game of Thrones* is based on medieval Europe, its themes of institutional corruption, political uncertainty and apocalyptic futures appeal to fans all over the world. In 2012, between the second and third seasons, the online magazine *Vulture* described its fanbase as the most devoted of all 'because of the sheer surging might and immediacy of its readers' (and viewers') obsessiveness over a story that is still in the midst of unfolding'.[12] George R. R. Martin, the author of the book series 'A Song of Ice and Fire' on which the television show is based, has found the attention problematic. In 2019, he said he had made a point of steering clear of the relentless online discussions about it because he feared they might distort his ideas about how the story should evolve. 'You can't please everybody,' he told the *Observer*, 'so you've got to please yourself.'[13]

A dedicated fan base raises the stakes for a screenwriter tasked with adapting a popular work for television or cinema. Jane Goldman, who has co-written the screenplays for much-loved films including the comic book adaptations *Kick-Ass* and *X-Men: First Class*, told me that she takes that responsibility very seriously, particularly because, as a fan herself (of Boy George, *The X-Files* and World of Warcraft, among other things), she knows what it's like to feel passionately about a story or a character. 'I'm always thinking about not wanting to sully something that somebody else loves, and wanting to be true to the spirit of it. I think about what would trouble me if this was my fandom.' For example, if a character has to die – a potentially traumatizing scenario for fans, as we'll soon learn – she has found that people don't mind so much if it fits the context of the story. 'But fans can smell if it's cheap or unjustified or if it's unearned. And that really holds authors accountable.'

In 2017, Goldman wrote the pilot for a *Game of Thrones* spin-off set thousands of years before the main series. Her brief was to chronicle the world's descent from a golden age of heroes to its darkest hour, a period known as the Long Night. Although the concept came from George R. R. Martin himself, he had written very little about it, so Goldman had to create the characters, the scenes and the storyline from scratch. At the time, the production company was exploring several different prequel ideas. Goldman says she was drawn to the Long Night because she wanted to explore a world that hadn't already been built and, in a way, claimed. 'The level of passion among *Game of Thrones* fans is so high and I was reticent to step into the canon that everyone knows,' she says. 'But working on something that was adjacent to that universe, with the blessing and involvement of George R. R. Martin, I wouldn't be treading on anybody's expectations. That was the only arena I felt comfortable in.'

In the end, after making the pilot, HBO decided not to take the Long Night prequel further. As a *Game of Thrones* fan myself, this feels like a missed opportunity – but you can't please all the fans all the time.

———

Being a fan is full of risk. Your friends and family might regard you as strange. There's a high chance you'll be disappointed by the storyline of your favourite show. There's also the possibility that your hero might die (unless you choose one who is immortal). This is rarely considered until it happens, but when it does it can hit hard. The death of a favourite star can feel like the death of a close friend or a family member. You may have felt this way when David Bowie, Prince, Robin Williams, Amy Winehouse or Elvis passed away. The grieving process can be intense and prolonged. In 2020, a group of researchers interviewed fans of Bowie, Michael Jackson and George Michael, who died in 2016, 2009 and 2016 respectively. Many of them recalled feeling 'devastated' at the time, as if their world had 'completely shattered'. They found a variety of ways to cope, such as connecting with other fans, enlarging their collection of memorabilia, or even making a shrine in their home. But they admitted that several years on, they still felt like crying when they talked about it, and worried that they would never get over it.[14]

It is easy to scoff, but these kinds of reactions are understandable when you consider that the majority of fans join a fandom when they are relatively young. We love our heroes not just for what they do but for what they represent, what they mean to us. They become our role models, and when we lose them, we lose some part of ourselves. The fact that we have probably never met them and our relationship with them is 'parasocial' rather than real is hardly relevant. 'It feels like the soundtrack of my life has ended,' one long-time Michael Jackson fan told the psychologist Gayle Stever after his death.[15]

Stever had conducted a study of Jackson fans seventeen years earlier, and after he died some of them reconnected with her on Facebook. 'They were basically looking for people to grieve with,' she says. 'They said, "We knew you'd understand."' Psychologists have found that social media plays an important role in helping fans cope with the death of a favourite celebrity.[16] By turning private grief into a public ritual, it allows them to connect with other people who 'get it', and to share their pain.[17] (Studies have shown that at times of tragedy, having other people around to supervise your sadness generally leads to a healthier outcome.) On 10 January 2016, the day Bowie lost his fight against cancer, fans paid their respects by sending more than 2.3 million tweets with the hashtag #RIPDavidBowie (at its peak, this reached 20,000 every minute).[18] This is the modern way, but it is not the only way. That same night, thousands of people gathered on the streets of Brixton in South London, where Bowie grew up, to sing his songs, leave flowers and write epitaphs on the wall opposite the Tube station. Unlike the tweet cascade, this impromptu wake had a lasting impact, turning the neighbourhood into a permanent memorial and a pilgrimage destination for Bowie's fans.

The death of a hero is unsettling, and no less so if the hero happens to be fictional. Beloved characters from literature and film find their way into our hearts and minds just as real people do. They become our friends, and when they die their loss can leave an unexpected void. Several *Harry Potter* fans I know were distraught at the demise of Albus Dumbledore, Fred Weasley, Severus Snape, Dobby the House Elf and other characters who they had come to like. My niece Flora, who describes the world of Harry Potter as her 'whole life' when she was nine and ten, remembers being horrified at the death of Sirius Black, a kindly father figure to Harry whose murder by his hated cousin Bellatrix Lestrange took all readers by surprise. 'It was very emotional,' she recalls. 'Tears were coming out!' The death of Fred Weasley, one of the elder brothers of Harry's best friend Ron, also hit hard, she says, 'because he was a twin and only one of them died. I feel it would almost have been better if they had died together.'

Thankfully, traumatic deaths are not common in the Harry Potter series, and most of them happen towards the end of the last book. Not so in *Game of Thrones*, which deserves its reputation as one of the deadliest shows on television. A staggering 6,887 characters died during the course of the eight seasons, almost all of them violently.[19] No one was safe: much-loved protagonists were regularly killed off in the middle of their lives. Fans of the series came to accept this precarious reality, yet some of the deaths still caused great sadness. An analysis of tweets posted in the ten days after the murder of Jon Snow at the end of season five (he was later resurrected) indicated that many viewers passed through the five stages of Elisabeth Kübler-Ross's classic model of grief: denial, anger, bargaining, sadness and acceptance.[20] As the show progressed and the body count continued to grow, the online magazine *Slate* opened a 'virtual graveyard', where fans could mourn their dead heroes by leaving a flower on their digital graves.[21]

Parasocial bereavement is not a symptom of a modern cultural malaise, as some have suggested. It has a long history. In 1893, when Arthur Conan Doyle had tired of his literary creation Sherlock Holmes after six years of adventures, he wrote a final instalment in which the detective fell to his death while fighting his arch-enemy Professor Moriarty. After the story was published in *The Strand Magazine*, he was astonished by the reaction. More than twenty thousand people cancelled their subscriptions to the periodical in protest. Some sent him hate mail. Legend has it that readers in London wore black armbands as a sign of their grief. Eight years later, conceding that he had underappreciated the popularity of his famous detective, Doyle brought him back, and Holmes has lived on in films, television adaptations, radio dramas, plays and video games.

How do characters who have never lived become so real? Why do they matter to us so much? In 2019, researchers at Erasmus University in Rotterdam asked fifteen fans of 'deceased' fictional characters how they had processed their grief and whether they took anything meaningful from their deaths. One of them, a young woman who had been particularly affected by the loss of Sirius Black in *Harry Potter*, had this to say:

> You see how someone develops. When you get to know someone's layers, in different situations, you get attached to these people. You form a connection, you know? The longer you follow someone, know someone . . . It just becomes real.[22]

It's hardly surprising that she cares so much. If you are a fan of anything – a fictional character, a celebrity, a sports team – what happens to them to some extent happens to you too. Your self-esteem and sense of identity are tied to their success; you are vulnerable to their misfortunes. This is why some sports fans have a second team that they can turn to if their main one fails, and why some even bet against their team to off-set the potential emotional hit of losing.[23] It is why all fans suffer some cognitive dissonance when their heroes transgress or behave in a way that conflicts with their own core values. It can be disorientating when someone you love or identify with lets you down. Since J. K. Rowling started sharing her controversial views about trans women – she believes that trans activism is eroding the rights and threatening the safety of cis-gender women – some of the Harry Potter fans who disagree with her have vowed never again to read her books or watch the films. They have become reluctant anti-fans, and not without considerable sorrow at the loss of a world that meant so much to them.

In a different corner of the moral universe, the #MeToo movement has encouraged many people to reassess their parasocial relationships with celebrities who have been accused of sexual misconduct. Is it possible to remain a fan of Woody Allen's films despite the allegation that he molested his young daughter? Is it permissible? In the absence of judicial finality, there is no framework that would allow fans to doubt the accused while continuing to appreciate their art. Often the art gets erased along with them.

It doesn't have to be that way. Emily Nussbaum, the television critic of the *New Yorker*, has suggested that we should be able to separate the creator from their work without forgiving them. She argues that it would be 'nuts' for her, an arts critic who grew up believing in the genius of Woody Allen, to never again make reference to *Manhattan* or *The Purple Rose of Cairo*, even though the films are saturated with his behaviour. 'Decent people sometimes create bad art,' she writes in her recent book *I Like to Watch*. 'Amoral people can and have created transcendent works. A cruel and selfish person – a criminal, even – might make something that was generous, life-giving, and humane. Or alternatively, they might create something that was grotesque in a way that you couldn't tear your eyes away from . . . History was full of such perversity.'[24]

––––––

In 2019, HBO and Channel 4 co-produced a documentary called *Leaving Neverland* about two men who claimed separately that they had been sexually molested as children by Michael Jackson. In the film, Wade Robson and James Safechuck describe how Jackson allegedly kissed and fondled them and performed acts of oral and anal sex on them while they were staying at his Neverland Ranch and in Los Angeles between 1988 and 1997, beginning when Robson was seven and Safechuck was ten. In both cases, the boys slept in Jackson's bedroom with the blessing of their mothers. '[Michael] was one of the kindest, most gentle, loving, caring people I knew,' says Wade. 'He helped me tremendously . . . He also sexually abused me for seven years.'

Jackson had already been accused of child molestation, in 1993 and again in 2003. The 1993 case, brought by thirteen-year-old Jordan Chandler and his family, was settled out of court with Jackson agreeing to pay $23 million; a criminal investigation was abandoned due to a lack of evidence. The 2003 accusations, which followed concerns raised in a controversial documentary that

Jackson regularly shared his bed with children, resulted in a criminal trial in 2005, where the singer was acquitted of all charges.

Against this background, *Leaving Neverland* was highly damaging to Jackson's reputation, ten years after his death. It was seen by millions of viewers around the world; in the UK, it was downloaded more times than any other programme in Channel 4's history. In the US it won an Emmy for Outstanding Documentary. It was also heavily criticized for being one-sided. Friends and supporters of Jackson accused the film's director Dan Reed of failing to investigate inconsistencies in the accounts of Safechuck and Robson, who had testified in Jackson's defence at his 2005 trial. They accused Reed of presenting Jackson as guilty without offering any independent evidence.

The documentary created a situation that was very uncomfortable for Jackson's fans. For a while, it was considered morally indefensible to endorse his artistic legacy, or even to admit to liking his music. A number of radio stations pulled his songs from their playlists. Members of one of the biggest Michael Jackson online communities reported that they were 'losing friends because of this whole *Leaving Neverland* mess'.[25] When some of his fans started to push back against the allegations, by accusing Reed of bias, or pointing out that Jackson had never been convicted by a court, many commentators treated them as transgressors and recycled old tropes about fans and dysfunctional behaviour. 'One can only compare them to religious fanatics, really,' Reed told the *New York Times*. 'They're the Islamic State of fandom.'[26]

Psychological studies have shown that people who identify strongly with celebrities find it easier to excuse them when they offend: they manage to 'decouple' their wrongdoings from their achievements. This may be why so many of Tiger Woods' admirers stuck with him after he admitted in 2009 to having had multiple extramarital affairs, and why the jersey of basketball star Kobe Bryant remained a top seller after he was charged with sexual assault in 2003.[27] One explanation is that impassioned fans have invested too much in the relationship to contemplate their idol's fall from grace: if I acknowledge that my role model is a sinner, where does that leave me? In the case of Michael Jackson, this seems too simplistic an analysis. Those fans who rallied against the media in the wake of *Leaving Neverland* were not seeking to excuse him – they simply didn't believe that the allegations against him were credible. 'His fans would be more willing to give him the benefit of the doubt than other people, for sure,' says Mark Duffett, who studies popular music fandoms at the University of Chester. 'But if there was cast-iron proof [that the allegations were true], I think you would find a mass defection from the fandom very quickly. Those people who are heavily invested in him would go through some kind of grieving process.'

Michael Jackson's fandom is one of the most diverse – in terms of age, socio-economic background, ethnicity and geography – of any global star. It is impossible to make general assumptions about why his fans love him, and about the myriad ways in which they responded to news of his alleged sexual misconduct. But one thing that unites them is the belief that Jackson was the target of racist abuse and unwarranted criticism throughout his career, and that the media that persecuted him during his lifetime cannot be trusted to tell the truth about him after his death.

In December 2020, I had several conversations with a long-time Michael Jackson fan who played a significant role in the campaign to counter the claims made in *Leaving Neverland*. Seán O'Kane was one of the founders of a crowdfunding initiative that placed adverts on the side of London buses and on bus shelters declaring Jackson 'innocent' alongside the slogan, 'Facts don't lie. People do.' They claimed to be 'an independent initiative helping the public to understand the facts and to reveal the truth in the false accusations against Michael Jackson'.[28]

O'Kane is in his late-thirties, affable and the father of a young son. He is a psychotherapist, specializing in sexual problems. He describes himself as an 'activist fan' rather than a superfan. He was drawn to Jackson not only for his music but also for his stance on environmental and humanitarian issues, and because he perceived him to be a victim of injustice. He grew up as a Catholic in Northern Ireland and his family, like many others, was deeply affected by the country's Troubles. Several of his relatives spent time in prison. As a teenager he became a peace ambassador, and visited the White House as part of a movement to promote inter-faith understanding. In fighting for Michael Jackson he felt he was taking a stand for civil rights, striking another blow against prejudice and discrimination.

Seán reminds me that since the mid-1980s the tabloids have often referred to Jackson as 'Wacko Jacko', a term with racist connotations and one the singer hated.[29] 'He was constantly the butt of jokes in the media.' They seemed to despise his extra-ordinary success as an entertainer, he says, and his savvy as a businessman (in 1985 Jackson acquired the publishing rights to the entire Beatles back catalogue). 'He was an easy target. It was like you could literally write what you wanted about him. He was a young black guy who was constantly being made fun of. That wouldn't happen today. He had a lot of flaws, but his flaws were so viciously exposed and dissected. He was tortured by the media.'

I discussed *Leaving Neverland* with a number of other Michael Jackson fans who did not wish to be identified for fear that they would become the targets of abuse on social media. Most of them expressed what sounded like discomfort mixed with resignation – discomfort at the idea that a lot of people who watched the documentary would find it convincing, resignation because 'we're used to negative media coverage, we're used to him not getting a fair trial'. Some, fearing that the allegations were true, seemed troubled at how that might affect their own identity: should they reject the man and keep the music, accept that he wasn't all good and live with the conflict, or scrub the relationship entirely – a disquieting prospect that would involve closing the door on an important part of their youth. One fan, a lawyer who had scrutinized the court papers from Jackson's 2005 trial and satisfied herself that he was innocent of those charges, was nonetheless clear where she stood should he turn out to be guilty in this case:

> I am not one of those people who can separate the man from the music. You hear that a lot – you know, can I still enjoy his music if he's a pedophile? No, you absolutely cannot. It's all or nothing for me. I'm not going to sing along about healing the world knowing he's done horrific things to a child.

As hard as we might try, it can be difficult to ignore what other people think of us and the things we cherish. After all, reputations count. Loyal fans often pretend to be impervious to criticism, but when public opinion turns against their idol – as it did with Michael Jackson – they are usually quick to defend them. This is true even for fans whose idol has been dead for more than five hundred years.

You'd be hard pushed to find an English historical figure with a worse reputation than Richard III. King of England for just over two years until his death at the Battle of Bosworth Field in 1485, he is popularly portrayed as a ruthless Machiavellian who stopped at nothing in his ambition to seize the throne. It is said that he was complicit in the deaths of a number of his relatives and close associates, among them the seventeen-year-old Prince of Wales, whose wife he then married; the prince's father Henry VI; his own brother the Duke of Clarence; his wife Anne, who he arranged to have poisoned; his trusted councillor Lord Hastings; and his young nephews Edward and Richard, who were smothered with a pillow while locked in the Tower of London. The fifteenth-century historian John Rous called Richard a 'tyrant, born under a hostile star', accusing him of ruling 'like the Antichrist'.[30] Sir Thomas More, writing a couple of generations after Richard's death,[31] found him 'close and secret, a deep dissembler, lowly of countenance, arrogant of heart, outwardly companionable where he inwardly hated, not hesitating to kiss whom he thought to kill, pitiless and cruel'.[32] His physical attributes were reputedly as crooked as his character. More depicts him as having 'a deformed body', with one shoulder higher than the other, and 'a short face and a cruel look, which did betoken malice, guile, and deceit'.[33] Historians over the centuries have whittled this description into a defining epithet: the Hunchback King.

This unfortunate rendering was hammered into the public consciousness by William Shakespeare in his play *Richard III*. Shakespeare's protagonist is a duplicitous hunchback with a withered arm, a 'poisonous bunch-backed toad'.[34] In Richard's opening speech, we learn of his bitterness . . .

> But I, that am not shaped for sportive tricks,
> Nor made to court an amorous looking-glass;
> I, that am rudely stamped, and want love's majesty
> To strut before a wanton ambling nymph;[35]

his ghastly physique . . .

> Cheated of feature by dissembling Nature,
> Deformed, unfinished, sent before my time
> Into this breathing world, scarce half made up,
> And that so lamely and unfashionable
> That dogs bark at me as I halt by them;[36]

and the path he intended to follow to the throne . . .

> I am determined to prove a villain
> And hate the idle pleasures of these days.
> Plots have I laid, inductions dangerous,
> By drunken prophecies, libels and dreams,
> To set my brother Clarence and the king
> In deadly hate the one against the other:[37]

Shakespeare's portrait of the king has dominated history books and school curricula for over four hundred years. 'His audacity and unscrupulousness were matched with a cunning and hypocrisy such as are seldom found united in one man,' pronounced *Chambers' Encyclopaedia* in 1895. The *Collins National Encyclopedia* that accompanied me through my early school years summed him up as having 'usurped the crown from his nephew, whom he is believed to have had murdered'. The current *Oxford Dictionary of National Biography*, while kinder on his character, still describes his seizing of the throne as 'profoundly shocking'.

Over the years, various commentators have questioned this version of history. In 1768, the politician and writer Sir Horace Walpole published *Historic Doubts on the Life and Reign of King Richard III*, in which he claimed that the accusations against the king 'rest on the slightest and most suspicious ground, if they rest on any at all'.[38] Walpole believed that the stories of Richard's treachery were fabricated by supporters of the Tudor king Henry VII, Richard's rival and successor, and that most of the crimes attributed to him were implausible. He also doubted the extent of his physical deformities, drawing attention to alternative perspectives: 'The old Countess of Desmond, who had danced with Richard, declared he was the handsomest man in the room except his brother Edward, and was very well made.'[39]

Jane Austen was sympathetic to Richard, at least when she was a teenager. In *The History of England*, part of her 'Juvenilia' collection of plays and short stories, she generously gives him the benefit of the doubt as a member of the House of York:

> The Character of this Prince has been in general very severely treated by Historians, but as he was a *York*, I am rather inclined to suppose him a very respectable Man. It has indeed been confidently asserted that he killed his two Nephews and his Wife, but it has also been declared that he did not kill his two Nephews, which I am inclined to believe true; and if this is the case, it may also be affirmed that he did not kill his Wife.[40]

In modern times, Richard's cause has been taken up by the Richard III Society, a group formerly known as the Fellowship of the White Boar (named after his personal heraldic symbol). The fellowship was founded in 1924 by a Liverpool surgeon called Saxon Barton – a wonderfully medieval name – and a small group of friends who believed that history had been unfair to the king. In 1959 it reconstituted itself as a society, presumably to make it sound less like a cult. Jeremy Potter, chairman of the society between 1971 and 1989, characterized a typical member at that time as a 'young, intelligent, left-handed, female librarian'[41] – though in my interactions with the group I have not encountered anyone fitting that description. The society has around 3,500 members, compared with just 200 in 1960. A recent survey suggests that around 70 per cent are female, three-quarters are retired and only a handful are under the age of forty-five.[42]

On 20 February 2021 I attended the society's AGM, via Zoom. An impressive 312 people joined the call from their libraries, kitchens and sitting rooms. Most were not yet up to speed with the finer points of video conferencing – the mute button seemed particularly challenging. There were sounds of food being eaten, a dog barking, people bickering with their partners. A grandfather clock chimed. 'Hello, can anyone hear me?' shouted one gentleman repeatedly, until the society's treasurer John Whiting assured him that we could, though we didn't really want to. Levity aside, the meeting was striking for the geographical diversity of the participants. The society's membership extends to thirty-one countries, and people had dialled in from Sydney, Oklahoma, Houston, Panama, Montreal, the Philippines, Germany, New Zealand and many parts of the UK. In his lifetime, Richard's fanbase was mostly in the north of England; today it is almost as international as Michael Jackson's.

The society's aim is to 'encourage and promote a more balanced view' of Richard III's character. Its party line on his legitimacy is that his accession to the throne was lawful and approved by Parliament, despite him imprisoning his nephew Edward V, the next in line. On his conduct, it maintains that he was a conscientious ruler who strengthened England's legal system; that he was brave in battle (even his enemies agreed with this); that he almost certainly did not kill his brother, his wife, the Prince of Wales or Henry VI; that the fate of his nephews is still a mystery; and that he has been unfairly judged by history.

Most members, who call themselves Ricardians, do not categorize themselves as 'fans' of Richard – they prefer to see themselves as part of an academic reappraisal of their hero. But their attitude towards him and the dynamics of the group have much in common with other fandoms. The society began as a fellowship, and it remains one in all but name. At first glance, its members appear to share little with each other, apart from an interest in medieval history and a disaffection for Zoom. But they are united by a feeling that a terrible injustice has been done to Richard's name, and a desire to set the record straight.

Why are they so certain that he has been maligned? More curiously, why do they care so much? 'I was taught at school that Richard III was the evil king and a hunchback and all the rest of it, but the more I read about him, the more I thought, "Hang on, this isn't right,"' explained John Whiting a few weeks after the AGM. 'I wanted to be sure what really happened. Unlike some members, I don't believe Richard was a misunderstood saint. He was a product of his times. But there's a lot to show that in the two and a bit years he was king, he achieved a phenomenal amount. The loyalty he showed before he became king towards his brother Edward IV is quite something. He was quite a guy. He was also a phenomenal warrior.'[43]

Sally Henshaw first suspected she was being sold a lie at the age of seventeen, when she travelled to Stratford to see a performance of Shakespeare's play. 'I thought, "Rattling good play, but hang on a minute, no one could be that evil. He couldn't have murdered his way to the throne." So I started researching that period and saw that Shakespeare's version wasn't accurate.' Sally has been a member of the Richard III Society for forty years. She is the secretary of the Leicester branch, and much of her social life revolves around it. She told me that while all Ricardians share an interest in Richard, 'their outlook on life and their ideas of history and what society is or should be are often completely different. Some of them can tell you what Richard was doing every day of his life but are not particularly interested in that period of history. Some like the social side, meeting up with others and forming friendships. Others are on a crusade: they want to clear Richard's name and if possible have him made into a saint.'

Most of the Ricardians I spoke with enjoy the idea that they are fighting for the underdog, and that history, which is generally written by professionals, is in this case being overwritten by amateurs. History is also written by the victors. Like Walpole, Ricardians believe that their man's reputation was besmirched by the Tudors who ousted him. Henry VII succeeded Richard after defeating him at Bosworth, but at least two dozen people had just as good a claim to the throne as he did. Henry's people, it seems, decided that the best way to cement his legitimacy was to paint his predecessor as a depraved thug, a narrative that John Rous, Thomas More and Shakespeare were only too happy to buy into.

If the tussle over Richard's reputation feels familiar, it may be because it has much in common with some of the themes of today's political culture. 'What happened with Richard in the Tudor period was the fake news and cancel culture of the time,' says Narrelle Harris, a Melbourne-based writer of crime, horror and fantasy fiction. As an Australian republican, she is not a fan of monarchy, but she has planted her flag in Richard III's camp 'because I can see it was such a miscarriage of justice. I don't think he was a saint, but Jesus, his press has been bad!' Like the writers of fan fiction we met in Chapter 3, Harris writes stories inspired by her heroes, including Sherlock Holmes. True to her fannish sensibilities, she has channelled her sympathies for the maligned king into a short story in which Shakespeare's villainous Richard III meets the equally villainous superhuman Khan Noonien Singh from *Star Trek* (as played by Benedict Cumberbatch in the 2013 film *Star Trek Into Darkness*). The story explores possible vulnerabilities in both characters that are only hinted at in the authorized versions, such as Richard's loveless childhood, that may explain their roguish behaviours. This being fantasy, the approach is more 'anatomical' than traditional treatments of Richard's character (squeamish members of the Richard III Society may want to look away):

Richard's one good arm let the dagger fall and he wound his arm around Khan's waist and tugged him impatiently closer. Richard was braced for the recoil, or for blows, and neither came. Instead, Khan fitted himself more closely in Richard's grip, and now deepened the kiss.[44]

———

In campaigning for a more balanced characterization of its hero, the Richard III Society has accomplished a great deal in his name. Its primary task is to promote research into his life and times, which it does through a grant scheme and its academic journal *The Ricardian*, and by encouraging collaborations between scholars. Thanks to these efforts, the late Middle Ages – and particularly the Wars of the Roses and the early years of the Tudor dynasty – is one of the best-studied periods of English history. The society has thirty local branches around the UK, and more overseas, each of which runs its own programme of talks and events. There being no Hampshire branch, I joined the one in London, whose programme for 2020 included lectures on the role of French convicts at the Battle of Bosworth; the use of propaganda during the Wars of the Roses; the menu at Richard's coronation banquet, which included peacock, swan and pike;[45] and, most ambitious of all, a project by a team of linguistics and vocal experts to recreate the sound of Richard's voice, based on what is known about the structure of his skull, his overall health, his posture and his personality.[46]

The enthusiasm of Ricardians for their subject has ensured that, more than five centuries after his death, the king is often in public view.[47] Social media users can follow his movements via the @RIII_Itinerary Twitter account, which helpfully tells us where he was and what he was doing on any given day. It is oddly comforting to know that on 20 June 1484 Richard III was in York, and that the next day he was in Pontefract, and that on 14 July he was back in York again. The most important day in the Ricardian calendar is 22 August, the anniversary of his death, which is commemorated each year at a service in Leicester Cathedral and at the nearby Bosworth battlefield site, where medievalists wearing chainmail armour and steel helmets re-enact his brave and fatal charge into the middle of the Tudor army. Each year on this day Ricardians travel to Leicester to honour their hero, and the Richard III Society sometimes requests an in memoriam notice in *The Times* or the *Daily Telegraph*, lest anyone be in any doubt about what happened:

PLANTAGENET Richard. Remember forever our good King Richard III, who fell at Bosworth Field 22nd August 1485. Betrayed, maligned, beloved by many.

After the Battle of Bosworth, Richard's body was hastily buried in a church in Leicester, without coffin or shroud. The whereabouts of his grave were soon forgotten. Its sensational discovery beneath a car park in September 2012 made headlines around the world. The story was all the more remarkable for the ignominious setting and for the revelation – gasp! – that his skeleton was deformed. Forensic analysis concluded that he had severe scoliosis, a form of spinal curvature that caused him to carry his right shoulder higher than his left – a conspic-uous irregularity, though hardly 'bunch-backed' as Shakespeare had claimed. The analysis also revealed that he suffered a savage death. His skull showed evidence of multiple wounds, including a blow from an axe-headed pole that sliced off part of the back of his head. There seems little doubt that he went down fighting.

The search for Richard's grave, which is dramatized in Stephen Frears' recent feature film *The Lost King*, was conceived and led by Philippa Langley, a writer and television producer who is also secretary of the Scottish branch of the Richard III Society. Like others, she hesitates to describe herself as a 'fan' of the king, though she doesn't hide her sympathies. '[He] was a man of good reputation, a skilled arbitrator and respected dispenser of justice,' she writes in *The King's Grave*, her book about the project. 'Shakespeare's evil and misshapen tyrant, and the psychotic murderer beloved of Tudor writers, should now be seen as a great dramatic invention.'[48] In a Channel 4 documentary about the excavation, she appears distressed when his skeleton is found 'hunched' in his grave, and again during the discussion of the injuries he received in battle. 'I don't see bones on that table – I see a man,' she declares at one point. She had spent nearly a decade researching Richard's life, and she felt she knew him pretty well. For her, as for many Ricardians, it was personal.[49]

Langley is now working on a project to solve the mystery of who, if anyone, killed the princes in the Tower, using forensic science and searching previously untapped archives. It's not hard to imagine which way this might go. I asked her, via email, whether she anticipated finding a definitive answer. 'Yes,' she replied. 'You have to understand that there is no evidence that the sons of Edward IV were murdered, in the Tower or anywhere else, or that Richard (or anyone else) was the perpetrator.' She added that she felt she was doing a job 'that our historians should have been doing all these centuries, but they just kept repeating Shakespeare's dramatic narrative'. If she can prove Richard's innocence, she hopes she will have done enough to finally lay the king to rest.[50]

Facial reconstruction of Richard III created from his skull by forensic anthropologist Caroline Wilkinson, commissioned by the Richard III Society. (© The Richard III Society. Reproduced by permission of the Society.)

In March 2015, Richard III was reburied in Leicester Cathedral with all the pomp and ceremony deserving of a medieval monarch (though without his feet, which the archaeologists were never able to find). Seven hundred members of the Richard III Society attended the rituals, along with bishops, archbishops, members of the royal family and a significant proportion of Leicester's population. The king is something of a folk hero in the city: streets and pubs are named for him, and white roses are often left at the feet of his statue outside the cathedral. A few days after the burial, with residents buzzing from the media attention, the city's football team began a winning streak that took them from the bottom of the league to the top of the Premiership the following year. Ricardians were not the only ones to credit their hero with a small role in that unlikely success story.

Richard's original burial site in the car park is preserved beneath a glass floor in what is now the King Richard III Visitor Centre. It may be the most important pilgrimage site for Ricardians: the cramped hole where he lay with his head on his shoulder seems more symbolic than his final resting place. On a recent visit to the centre, two women waiting behind me politely declined the curator's offer of a guided talk, requesting instead 'a quiet moment by his grave'. Many Ricardians reach for an emotional connection, for reasons even they may not understand. What begins as a fight for reputation and historical accuracy ends with something far more mysterious.

This chapter has shown that the most embattled fans – those who feel compelled to defend their interests or the reputation of their hero – are often the most dedicated. If you find the commitment of the Ricardians or of Michael Jackson's fans puzzling, the fandoms we encounter in the final chapter may seem incredible to you. Their members specialize in murder. Despite the alarming subject matter, they are much like any other fans – though they feel the pull of the dark side more than most.

8

Monsters Like Us

THE HABIT OF GRAVITATING towards people who share our outlook comes as naturally to us as breathing. It is human psychology at its most elemental: it drives our behaviour without us having to think about it, regardless of our intentions, regardless of the outcome. The world would almost certainly be less divisive and less violent if we were not so disposed. But it would also lack fandoms.

This psychological backstory helps explain why there exists a special interest group for just about every cultural phenomenon you care to think of, and why, alongside fandoms that celebrate heroic figures and popular narratives, there are 'dark' fandoms in which people come together to share their fascination for death and suffering. At first glance, dark fandoms seem very different from the ones we've considered so far, and yet they are surprisingly similar. People are drawn to them for the same reasons they are drawn to Jane Austen or *Game of Thrones*. And despite the gruesome subject matter, their members are not – with some worrying exceptions – the depraved psychopaths they are often assumed to be.

It can be hard to get your head around the idea that someone might look favourably on Eric Harris and Dylan Klebold, the twelfth-graders who murdered twelve of their fellow students and a teacher at Columbine High School in Colorado on 20 April 1999. They shot most of their victims at close range, in some cases taunting them as they died, before eventually turning their guns on themselves. If the bombs they had planted in the school cafeteria had detonated as planned, they would have killed hundreds more. At the time it was the deadliest school shooting in US history. They spent a year planning it. Their final messages were full of hate, for their fellow students and humanity. In a video filmed shortly before the massacre, they talked of their desire to start a 'revolution of the dispossessed'. 'You guys will all die, and it will be fucking soon,' says Harris in the film, to which Klebold adds, 'I hope we kill 250 of you.'[1]

Believe it or not, Harris and Klebold have thousands of fans, who call themselves 'Columbiners'. They are not the only mass killers to have their own followings: Dylann Roof, the white supremacist who shot nine members of a Black church in Charleston, South Carolina, in 2015, has 'Roofies'; James Holmes, who murdered twelve people at a movie theatre in Aurora, Colorado, in 2012, has 'Holmies'. But in this strange subculture, Harris and Klebold are the main draw. Their crime has been the reference point, and in some cases the inspiration, for almost all subsequent school shootings.

The Columbine High School massacre has gained special prominence because it was the first to be extensively covered by the media (its latter stages were broadcast live on television), and because a vast amount of information about it is available to the public. If you are so inclined, you can watch videos of Harris and Klebold testing their weapons in the woods, read extracts from their journals and schoolwork, reflect on their tastes in music or gawp at a photograph of their suicide. The event has been incorporated into popular culture: it features in numerous films, television dramas, songs, books and video games. 'Doing a Columbine' has become a euphemism for any 'lone actor' terror attack. The legacy of that April day has become impossible to ignore.

The majority of people who idolize Harris and Klebold neither condone what they did nor wish to emulate them.[2] There is no evidence that they are mentally disturbed (like Klebold) or psychopathic (like Harris – though these diagnoses are speculative). On the spectrum of psychological subtypes, they rate fairly normal. They tend to be nonchalant about their involvement in the fandom. 'We have our interests and you have yours, ours is just a little different,' one of them commented on Tumblr.[3] Another fan, in an interview with psychologists, explained that they found Harris and Klebold easy to relate to:

> The characters they played to the world were cool bad guys. I'm sure in real life they were nerdy, geeky and not as cool as they pass themselves off as, but many people, kids especially, can see themselves as either them or friends of theirs. They like the same music, play the same games.[4]

Many Columbiners have in common a narrative of social trauma. In comments on Tumblr, Facebook and Reddit, they describe how they have been bullied or ostracized by their peers, and how difficult this has made their lives. They appear to empathize with the shooters as fellow victims. Harris and Klebold implied in their journals and films that they had been picked on by jocks at their school. 'You've been giving us shit for years,' says Klebold in their final video. Bullying and social rejection are unlikely to have been the only contributing factors behind their actions, or even the main ones; many school shooters – including, apparently, Harris and Klebold – suffer from narcissistic personality traits and depression.[5] But several studies have shown that teenagers who have an interest in school shootings or who threaten to carry one out themselves are significantly more likely to have been the victims of bullying than teenagers in general.[6] It is certainly the dominant storyline in the fandom. 'I get sad every time I think how dylan and eric were treated,' declared one Columbiner on Tumblr recently. Another fan somewhat perversely likened them to Christ: '[Jesus] was the Dylan Klebold of his junior high . . . constantly bullied for being the only white kid in his school.'

In 2018, Jenni Raitanen and Atte Oksanen at the University of Tampere in Finland interviewed twenty-two people who had expressed a deep interest in school shootings on social media. Despite being from twelve different countries, the researchers found their narratives to be strikingly similar. They all talked extensively about how Harris and Klebold had been mistreated by their peers and how things might have turned out differently if they had been better understood. They spoke of the bullying and social exclusion that they themselves had endured, and frequently compared their own lives to the lives of the shooters. They identified with what they *perceived* to be Harris and Klebold's emotional experience, as these extracts from the interviews make clear.[7]

I only saw them as these two monsters that did this horrible thing, and as my research progressed, I saw they were just kids like me, who were bullied and isolated to the brink, and they snapped.

I've been severely bullied and beaten in school. Plus problems at home. And my own psychological problems. I can totally relate to what drives them to do something like that.

Most Columbiners have one thing in common: we have felt like outsiders or victims at some point in our lives. We have felt like absolutely nobody could understand how alone we have felt, and that experience is exactly what Eric and Dylan lived.

It is hard to understand why, out of all the bullied and persecuted characters in popular culture, anyone would choose as role models two people with such an extreme trajectory. Still, many Columbiners have found the connection helpful. It has made them feel less alone, given them a different perspective on their troubles or allowed them to find solutions without resorting to revenge (almost all the interviewees emphasized that while they felt a connection with the shooters, they did not identify with their actions). 'Knowing that there were even just two boys out there who felt the same way as we feel now gives us comfort,' one of them told the researchers.

Oksanen told me that he thought finding an online community was a positive step for their interviewees. 'For people who are socially excluded, isolated, feeling lonely or lacking friends, it is very difficult to share ideas offline, so to find similarly minded people online can be empowering. It must be a relief for them. For young people who have been consistently bullied over the years, you can certainly understand it.' At the same time, he worries that belonging to a group that routinely discusses extreme ideas might take some of them 'in the wrong direction'.

In lots of ways, the Columbiner community resembles many of the fandoms we have already met. It attracts people with a common backstory and with similar beliefs, values and attitudes. Its members connect with Harris and Klebold just as fans of popular culture connect with A-list celebrities or characters in their favourite novel. The ways in which they engage with their subject matter – the extensive research, the obsessing over detail, the delighting in previously unseen material – bring to mind the preoccupations of Trekkies or Potterheads. On the online forums where they communicate, there is endless speculation over why the bombs in the school cafeteria failed to explode (did Dylan tamper with them to save lives?), why the killers didn't murder more students when they had plenty of opportunities to do so (were they 'playing God'?), what happened to their bloodied T-shirts (were they returned to their families?), what happened to their bodies (is there a grave?), and so on. Some of them channel their fascination into drawings, photo montages, video remixes or other works of fan art which they share online. More than a few have 'Eric and Dylan' tattoos.

As you can imagine, Columbiners get a lot of hate, both from people who mistrust their motives and from others who believe it inappropriate for anyone to show Harris and Klebold compassion. This kind of thing:

The 'Columbiners fandom' has officially broken me and made me lose my faith in humanity and myself. Thanks a lot, you fucked up school shooter worshipping psychopaths![8]

In this regard, they are not dissimilar to therians, female gamers and Michael Jackson fans, all of whom have been on the receiving end of abundant abuse – though it is a lot easier to understand why anyone would despise Columbiners. They are fortunate to be part of a fandom: embattled communities tend to pull together. It's far easier to face derision with others than on your own.[9]

———

In one very important way, school-shooter subcultures are quite different from traditional fandoms: a tiny minority of their members aspire to be mass murderers. Although the risk is low, there is no doubt that people with a deep and protracted interest in school shootings are more likely to try to carry one out.

Columbine inspired at least twenty-one shootings and fifty-three thwarted plots in the US between 1999 and 2014, according to an investigation by reporters at the American magazine *Mother Jones*.[10] Many of the perpetrators explicitly referred to Harris and Klebold in their writings or videos or copied their clothing, behaviour and tactics. Cho Seung-hui, who killed thirty-two students at the Virginia Tech campus in Virginia in 2007, said he wanted to 'repeat Columbine', and in his final manifesto described himself as a martyr 'like Eric and Dylan'. Adam Lanza, who wreaked carnage in 2012 at Sandy Hook Elementary School (all but six of his twenty-six victims were aged six or seven), owned hundreds of documents, pictures and videos relating to Columbine. He was also a regular contributor to a Columbine-related online forum and had put together a detailed spreadsheet with information on five hundred mass murderers and the weapons they used.

The 'copycat effect' is common among all mass-killers who

are not part of a terrorist organization. Peter Langman, a psychologist who specializes in this type of crime, has identified fifty-seven cases between 1966 and 2017 where a lone shooter was inspired by previous killers. 'Having a role model or an ideology that supports their violent intentions may [transform] what is otherwise aberrant and abhorrent into something admirable,' he explained in his study. 'It validates, or legitimates, the urge toward violence.'[11]

On 15 March 2019, a couple of months after Langman published his analysis, a twenty-eight-year-old white supremacist called Brenton Tarrant killed fifty-one people and injured forty others during Friday prayers at two mosques in Christchurch, New Zealand. In his manifesto – a long-winded rant against immigrants and 'enemies of our race' – he claimed he had been influenced by Dylann Roof and other school shooters, and particularly by the far-right Norwegian terrorist Anders Breivik. (Breivik was also idolized by Adam Lanza and a number of other school shooters.)[12] On the far-right internet forum 8chan, white supremacists lauded Tarrant for his actions. 'Brenton Tarrant did what everyone on this board only dreams about. He took the fight to the enemy and won . . . This is only the beginning,' wrote one anonymous contributor.[13] Tarrant was subsequently cited as an inspiration in four separate extremist attacks that took place in California, Texas, Norway and Germany that same year.[14] This grim cycle, in which each killer is viewed as a martyr by the next, shows no sign of letting up. Since 2012, extremists have plotted or carried out an average of twenty attacks each year in the US. Almost all of them were linked to white supremacists or other right-wing radicals.[15]

Copycat killers do not have to look very hard to find

information about their heroes, and there is no shortage of ways for them to broadcast their own ideas and crimes. Tarrant live-streamed part of his massacre on Facebook via a helmet-mounted GoPro camera, and copies of this video have been widely shared online. The mainstream media shows little restraint in its reporting of mass killings. This is significant: copycat cases are more likely when an event receives extensive coverage, particularly if it ended in a suicide.[16] Atte Oksanen, the Finnish researcher who studies school shootings, thinks it would be preferable if the media didn't report on them at all – the less material that is made public, the better. This would also prevent shooters from achieving the notoriety they crave.

School-shooter fandoms, including Columbiners, almost certainly contribute to the copycat effect. Graphic information about mass murders is routinely shared on their forums, with little oversight. 'Most of these people do not become perpetrators themselves, but there are still some who are more at risk, and the fact this community exists is supporting the whole phenomenon,' Oksanen says.

How should moderators go about spotting the small minority of enthusiasts who might be at risk of following the path set by Harris, Klebold, Breivik, Lanza, Tarrant and the rest? Scrutinizing message boards for extremist ideologies and beliefs is likely to be a waste of time, since 99 per cent of people with radical ideas never act on them. Attitudes do not easily translate into behaviours, and there is no straightforward route from extremist opinion to extremist deed.[17]

Lately, investigators have started using linguistic analysis to differentiate extremists who intend to use violence from those who are merely voicing radical thoughts. They focus on style rather than content and meaning – how someone uses 'function words' such as pronouns and prepositions that dictate the syntax of a sentence. The assumption is that planning and thinking about a violent act is cognitively stressful, and this mental strain is reflected in their language. In the lead-up to a violent act, people have been found to use more personal pronouns and an increasingly simplistic cognitive style involving fewer contradict-ory ideas. One advantage of taking a linguistic approach is that it is difficult for anyone to mask their intentions by consciously manipulating their syntax. Another is that since most extremist killers are active contributors to online fandoms and eager to share their thoughts on social media, there is no shortage of material to analyse.[18]

One of the difficulties of trying to understand school shooters and other so-called lone-actor terrorists is that they do not easily match a psychological profile. They are both alone and not alone. Since they do not belong to any terrorist group or political organ-ization, the decision to kill is entirely theirs. Yet they are connected by the weak ties of online community and radical ideology. They are strongly influenced by previous killers; they interact with fellow enthusiasts in online forums and they consolidate their views within broad networks of like-minded extremists. In his manifesto, Brenton Tarrant boasted that he had 'donated to many nationalist groups' and 'interacted with many more'. A couple of years before his attacks against Muslims in Christchurch, he spent several months travelling in Europe, visiting sites of histor-ical clashes between Orthodox Christians and Ottoman Turks in a kind of anti-fan pilgrimage. His social ties extended both outwards in space and backwards in time.[19]

Still, Tarrant was more alone than most people. Like many

lone-actor killers, he lacked a meaningful social group that might have regulated his anger and tested the appropriateness of his outlook. Psychological studies of such terrorists have consistently found evidence in their life stories of isolation or social disconnection.[20] Some of them are inhibited from building stronger ties by their introverted or neurotic personalities; others are cold-shouldered by radical groups because of their impulsivity or extreme ideas. They are fans without a fandom. Ostracized even by those who share their views, they end up seeking recognition in the bleakest way possible.

———

Mass killers are a niche fandom. Serial killers, on the other hand, get a much better press. Somehow, it is more acceptable to be interested in someone who murders his victims one at a time than one who murders them all at once. The lives of serial killers, popularized in films, TV shows, exhibitions and 'true crime' podcasts, have come to resemble monstrous fairy tales. Outwardly, they appear impossibly normal. They might have families, jobs and a rich social life. They can be charismatic and neighbourly, which makes them hard to catch. And they almost always kill people they don't know.[21] Many of us seem to find this an irresistible combination.

Over the winter of 1957–8, tens of thousands of Americans found it impossible to resist a visit to Plainfield, Wisconsin, where they could ogle at the home of Ed Gein, a reclusive bachelor who had recently been arrested for killing two women and digging up the corpses of several more. You could hardly blame them. Police had found a gallery of monstrosities in his house: the headless, disembowelled body of a local shop-owner hanging by her heels in the kitchen; a collection of female genitalia in an old shoebox; human skulls repurposed as soup bowls; a belt adorned with female nipples; a vest made from human skin. Who wouldn't be curious? In the years that followed, Gein inspired a succession of fictional killers, including Norman Bates in *Psycho*, Leatherface in *The Texas Chainsaw Massacre* and Buffalo Bill in *The Silence of the Lambs*. He was 'the patron saint of splatter, the grandfather of gore', as his biographer Harold Schechter put it.[22] It was hard to look away.

The modern fascination with serial killers has become so prevalent that it now passes as just another kind of media consumption, on a par with a love for science-fiction films or animé. But some fans seek a more extravagant level of engagement. Not satisfied with binge-watching slasher movies or rubber-necking at crime scenes, they yearn to touch the evil-doer, to scratch at the core of the horror. There are several ways to do this. You can exchange letters with killers in prison, or even speak with them on the phone (one fan in Pennsylvania played me a recording of a rambling conversation he'd had with the cult leader and convicted killer Charles Manson). Another strategy is to collect 'murderabilia', artefacts relating to killers and their crimes: paintings, scraps of handwriting, signed photographs, locks of hair.

In 2016, while researching an article about serial killers, I held the razor that Ed Gein supposedly used to skin his victims. It had somehow found its way to Steven Scouller, a Scottish collector who also owns Fred West's ID card and has a bundle of letters from Dennis Nilsen. It looked like any old razor except, well, it wasn't. Later, on a trip to New York, I visited the apartment of Joe Coleman, a painter who keeps a large collection of serial-killer ephemera and other relics of the profane in what he calls his

'Odditorium'. He pointed out a few of his favourite things. A bullet from the gun that killed Lee Harvey Oswald. A tuft of Charles Manson's hair. A painting by John Wayne Gacy, the children's entertainer who murdered dozens of boys in Chicago. A letter from the 'Brooklyn Vampire' Albert Fish to the mother of his final victim, Grace Budd; 'Dear Mrs Budd' it begins, before going on to describe how he cut up and ate her daughter, and what she tasted like.[23] The trade in murderabilia is worth millions of dollars a year. At the time of writing, on various obscure auction sites it was possible to bid for Dennis Nilsen's glasses (£2,000), a letter from Ted Bundy ($3,999), an oil painting by John Wayne Gacy ($175,000), a used prison toothbrush that belonged to Hadden Clark ($65) and Charles Manson's worn prison shorts ($850).[24]

The motives of people who buy such items are routinely questioned, but they seem surprisingly benign. They are collectors like any other. They mean no disrespect to the victims. Their interests tend to lie not in the killings but in the lives of the killers. Serial killers can appear spectacularly normal. What makes them capable of such horror? The question should concern all of us. Scouller told me that in his correspondence with Dennis Nilsen, he found him 'very articulate'. He went on: 'He seemed so tuned in to what was going on in the world. I read those letters and I thought, "You're clearly an intelligent person – you could have been anybody you want, but you went down this other road."' To be clear, that other road led to Nilsen killing at least twelve young men and boys and retaining their corpses in life-like poses in his flat while he chatted or had sex with them.

Is it so weird to speculate about what happened there? To ponder on the humanity and the deviance and how the two could live side by side? In serial-killer and school-shooter fandoms, there is little to celebrate, but there is a great deal to contemplate. It seems reasonable to ask what might have driven those people to commit such terrible crimes, and what would it have taken to send them down a different road.

Epilogue

T O BE A FAN means many things, but at its heart it is an act of love. The fans who feature in this book are remarkably diverse in their interests, ages, backgrounds and motivations, yet they are all committed to something beyond themselves. They are on a search for meaning, and they are prepared to give a great deal of themselves to find it.

For a good part of my teenage years I was a devoted fan of the rock band The Police, and in particular of their drummer Stewart Copeland. Naturally I owned every piece of music they produced, and many bootleg live recordings, and as a drummer myself I spent hours trying to replicate Stewart's idiosyncratic drum patterns. Recently I had a possibility of meeting him, via a mutual friend. After much deliberation I decided not to follow it through, thinking it could only disappoint. After all, he had given me so much already – how could I hope for more?

I realize now that my love for The Police was less than it could have been, not because it was unrequited or 'parasocial', but because I never found a way to share it. I didn't join a fan club or hang out with other worshippers at gigs (in the pre-internet era this was harder to do). I rather wish it had been otherwise. I've lost count of the number of fans who have told me that belonging to a fandom was the source of their greatest fulfilment, or the best thing that had ever happened to them. Still, it's never too late. You never know when you're going to fall for something or someone bigger than yourself. Next time, I'll be all in.

Selected Sources

Enterprising Women: Television fandom and the creation of popular myth, by Camille Bacon-Smith (University of Pennsylvania Press, 1991)

Playing to the Crowd: Musicians, audiences, and the intimate work of connection, by Nancy Baym (New York University Press, 2018)

A Companion to Media Fandom and Fan Studies, edited by Paul Booth (Wiley-Blackwell, 2018)

Henri Tajfel: Explorer of identity and difference, by Rupert Brown (Routledge, 2020)

Framing Fan Fiction: Literary and social practices in fan fiction communities, by Kristina Busse (University of Iowa Press, 2017)

The Fanfiction Reader: Folk tales for the digital age, by Francesca Coppa (University of Michigan Press, 2017)

Animals and Society: An introduction to human–animal studies, by Margo DeMello (Columbia University Press, 2012)

Fangirls: Scenes from modern music culture, by Hannah Ewens (Quadrille, 2019)

Fandom as Methodology: A sourcebook for artists and writers, edited by Catherine Grant and Kate Random Love (Goldsmiths Press, 2019)

Jane Austen: Her homes and her friends, by Constance Hill (John Lane, 1902)

Fic: Why fanfiction is taking over the world, by Anne Jamison (Smart Pop / BenBella Books, 2013)

Textual Poachers: Television fans and participatory culture, by Henry Jenkins (Routledge, 1992)

Fans, Bloggers and Gamers: Exploring participatory culture, by Henry Jenkins (New York University Press, 2006)

Jane Austen's Cults and Cultures, by Claudia Johnson (University of Chicago Press, 2012)

The King's Grave: The search for Richard III, by Philippa Langley and Michael Jones (John Murray, 2013)

The Adoring Audience: Fan culture and popular media, edited by Lisa Lewis (Routledge, 1992)

Austentatious: The evolving world of Jane Austen fans, by Holly Luetkenhaus and Zoe Weinstein (University of Iowa Press, 2019)

Fan Phenomena: Jane Austen, edited by Gabrielle Malcolm (Intellect Books, 2015)

I Like to Watch: Arguing my way through the TV revolution, by Emily Nussbaum (Random House, 2019)

Squee from the Margins: Fandom and race, by Rukmini Pande (University of Iowa Press, 2018)

Camp Austen: My life as an accidental Jane Austen superfan, by Ted Scheinman (Farrar, Straus and Giroux, 2018)

Real Characters: The psychology of parasocial relationships with media characters, ed. by Karen Shackleford (Fielding University Press, 2020)

SELECTED SOURCES

The Secret Lives of Sports Fans: The science of sports obsession, by Eric Simons (Overlook Duckworth, 2013)

The Psychology of Celebrity, by Gayle Stever (Routledge, 2019)

Human Groups and Social Categories: Studies in social psychology, by Henri Tajfel (Cambridge University Press, 1981)

Everything I Need I Get From You: How fangirls created the internet as we know it, by Kaitlyn Tiffany (MCD x FSG Originals, 2022)

Starlust: The secret lives of fans, by Fred and Judy Vermorel (W. H. Allen, 1985)

Sports Fans: The psychology and social impact of fandom, by Daniel Wann and Jeffrey James (Taylor and Francis, 2019)

Among the Janeites: A journey through the world of Jane Austen fandom, by Deborah Yaffe (Mariner, 2013)

Fandom at the Crossroads: Celebration, shame and fan/producer relationships, by Lynn Zubernis and Katherine Larsen (Cambridge Scholars, 2012)

Acknowledgements

THANK YOU TO ALL the fans (in the broadest definition of the term) who spoke to me for this book. I'm particularly grateful to Sophie Andrews, Abigail Rose and Amy Coombes of the Jane Austen Pineapple Appreciation Society; Leah Holmes, Laura Watton and Lisa-Jane Holmes of the Animé Babes; BearX, Azi, Lyc and the other therians who took something of a risk by agreeing to participate; Philippa Langley, John Whiting, Sally Henshaw and Stephen York of the Richard III Society; to Seán O'Kane, Thea Gundesen and Penelope Tubbs; and to the Potterheads in my family, who taught me everything I know about Harry's world.

Thank you to the writers, performers, guides and curators who shared their own perspectives on fandoms, including Lizzyspit, Cliff Jones, Jane Goldman, Don Short, Ben Thompson, Atlin Merrick, Narrelle Harris and Elizabeth Proudman, as well as Sophie Reynolds and Robert Booker and their colleagues at the wonderful Jane Austen's House Museum in Chawton.

Many of the theories in this book are based on the fascinating research of a number of psychologists and experts in fan culture, in particular Gayle Stever, Courtney Plante, Stephen Reysen, Kathleen Gerbasi, Elizabeth Fein, Helen Clegg, Stephen Reicher, Alex Haslam, Marilynn Brewer, Daniel Wann, Atte Oksanen, Lynn Zubernis, Katherine Larsen, Megan Knowles, Jaye Derrick, Mark Duffett and Brianna Dym.

Thank you to the friends and the friends of friends who introduced me to key characters or donated their time and expertise, especially Sabina ffrench Blake, Daisy Dunn, David Woodd, Yosh Kosminski and the much missed Michael Saunders.

Finally, special thanks to my editor Nick Humphrey; to my publisher Ravi Mirchandani and his incredible team at Picador, particularly Roshani Moorjani and Nicholas Blake; and to my agent Bill Hamilton for helping me develop the initial idea and more generally for keeping the whole show on the road.

Notes

CHAPTER I: A SOCIAL HISTORY OF FANDOMS

1   The London Library: www.londonlibrary.co.uk.

2   From Henry Dickens, *Memories of My Father* (Victor Gollancz, 1928), p. 17; via *Dickens: Interviews and Recollections*, ed. Philip Collins (Macmillan, 1981), volume 1, p. xvii.

3   The Sherlock Holmes stories were serialized between 1891 and 1927 in *The Strand Magazine*.

4   From John Dickson Carr, *The Life of Arthur Conan Doyle* (John Murray, 1949), p. 165. Other sources on the public appetite for Sherlock Holmes include Reginald Pound, *The Strand Magazine, 1891–1950* (Heinemann, 1966); and Ann McClellan, *Sherlock's World: Fan fiction and reimagining of BBC's Sherlock* (University of Iowa Press, 2018).

5   This derivation is related in Jerrold Casway, *The Culture and Ethnicity of Nineteenth Century Baseball* (McFarland, 2017), p. 59. Another theory is that 'fan' was an abbreviation of 'fancy', a much-used word in the eighteenth century denoting a follower of boxing, pigeoning or other pursuits.

6   Hugh Fullerton, 'Fans', *The American Magazine*, August 1910; sourced via Daniel Cavicchi, 'Foundational discourses of fandom', in *A Companion to Media Fandom and Fan Studies*, ed. Paul Booth (Wiley, 2018), ch. 2.

7   The rise of science-fiction fandoms in the 1920s, '30s and '40s is
     extensively documented in Sam Moskowitz, *The Immortal Storm: A
     history of science fiction fandom* (Hyperion Press, 1974); and Harry
     Warner, *All Our Yesterdays: An informal history of science fiction
     fandom in the forties* (Advent, 1969).

8   John Sullivan, *Media Audiences: Effects, users, institutions, and power*
     (Sage, 2013), p. 196.

9   Henry Jenkins (1988), '*Star Trek* rerun, reread, rewritten: fan writing
     as textual poaching', *Critical Studies in Media Communication* 5(2), pp.
     85–107.

10   Will Brooker, *Using the Force: Creativity, community and Star Wars
     fans* (Continuum, 2002), p. xii.

11   William Proctor (2013), '"Holy crap, more *Star Wars*! *More Star
     Wars*? What if they're crap?": Disney, Lucasfilm and *Star Wars*
     online fandom in the 21st Century', *Participations: Journal of Audience
     and Reception Studies* 10(1), pp. 198–224.

12   The study also found that a significant number of animé fans are
     non-binary, which suggests that male fans are in a minority. The
     research was part of Leah Holmes's thesis, which she hopes to
     publish as a book. She is currently building an archive of UK
     animé fandom from the pre-internet age to the present.

13   In Daniel Cavicchi, 'Loving music: listeners, entertainments, and the
     origins of music fandom in nineteenth-century America', in Jonathan
     Gray, Cornel Sandvoss and Lee Harrington, eds, *Fandom: Identities
     and communities in a mediated world* (New York University Press, 2017),
     p. 110.

14   Michael Mirer, Megan Duncan and Michael Wagner (2018), 'Taking
     it from the team: assessments of bias and credibility in team-
     operated sports media', *Newspaper Research Journal* 39(4), DOI:
     10.1177/0739532918806890. A separate study into the nature of
     political tribalism, published the following year, showed that
     liberals and conservatives exhibit similar levels of partisan bias and
     intolerance towards people with alternative views: Cory Clark et al.
     (2019), 'Tribalism is human nature', *Current Directions in
     Psychological Science* 28(6), pp. 587–92.

15 Before Napoleon, French citizens were obligated to serve by duty, money or servitude. For more details on how Napoleon raised his 'fan army', see Rupert Smith, *The Utility of Force: The art of war in the modern world* (Alfred Knopf, 2007), ch. 1.

16 Voter registration data from www.vote.org.

CHAPTER 2: THINK GROUP

1 Unbeknown to the boys, these criteria were a ruse: to ensure that the numbers in the groups were even, Tajfel secretly divided them up at random.

2 Henri Tajfel (1970), 'Experiments in intergroup discrimination', *Scientific American* 223(5), pp. 96–103.

3 Most previous studies of group conflict deliberately set groups against each other. One of the best known, referenced by Tajfel in his 1970 paper, was Muzafer Sherif's 1954 Robber's Cave experiment, in which he pitched two teams of adolescent boys in competition at a summer camp in Oklahoma and observed the tribal warfare that developed. For a full description, see http://psychclassics.yorku.ca/Sherif.

4 Michael Billig and Henri Tajfel (1973), 'Social categorization and similarity in intergroup behaviour', *European Journal of Social Psychology* 3, pp. 27–52.

5 Henri Tajfel, *Human Groups and Social Categories* (Cambridge University Press, 1981), p. 234.

Tajfel was a popular and controversial figure at Bristol. A former student told me, 'He had an incredible warmth that he could turn on and off. He could be wonderful to people and he could be disgraceful with people. His behaviour towards women was appalling.' A number of his female students accused him of sexual harassment. His most recent biographer, Rupert Brown, noted that Tajfel hardly ever addressed sexism or gender relations in his work. 'For someone whose antennae for problematic intergroup relations in the world were usually so finely tuned, is it not remarkable that he managed so completely to overlook this most fundamental of social fault-lines?' asked Brown. See Rupert Brown, *Henri Tajfel: Explorer of identity and difference* (Routledge, 2020).

6   In the 1970s, Tajfel and Turner developed 'social identity theory' to explain how people define themselves in terms of a shared social identity, and the effect that has on intergroup behaviours. Turner later built on these ideas with his 'self-categorization theory', which explores in greater depth the cognitive mechanisms through which people categorize themselves and others into groups; he famously argued that group behaviour is only possible because of our ability to take on a shared social identity. For purposes of simplification, I have treated these two theories as a unified theory, known generally as the 'social identity perspective'.

For more detail see Henri Tajfel and John Turner, 'An integrative theory of intergroup conflict', in W. Austin and S. Worchel, eds, *The Social Psychology of Intergroup Relations* (Brooks/Cole, 1979), pp. 33–47; and John Turner et al., *Rediscovering the Social Group: A self-categorization theory* (Blackwell, 1987). For a brief but comprehensive summary of social identity theory and self-categorization theory, see Alexander Haslam et al., 'The social identity perspective today: an overview of its defining ideas', in Tom Postmes and Nyla Branscombe, eds, *Rediscovering Social Identity* (Psychology Press, 2010), pp. 341–56.

7   Henri Tajfel, 'La catégorisation sociale', in S. Moscovici, ed., *Introduction à la Psychologie Sociale*, vol. 1 (Larousse, 1972), p. 275.

8   Skipping across group boundaries can also be transformative: while researching this book, I met a passionate fan of Rangers Football Club who had become good friends with a fan of Rangers' sworn rivals Celtic over their shared love of the music of Michael Jackson.

9   Tobia Schlager and Ashley Whillans (2022), 'People underestimate the probability of contracting the coronavirus from friends', *Humanities and Social Sciences Communications* 9, article 59.

10   Evidence for this comes from brain imaging studies that monitored people while they watched someone being pricked by a needle. When the person being pricked was a member of their in-group

(as opposed to an out-group), activity in those parts of their brain associated with pain and empathy, such as the anterior cingulate cortex and the anterior insula, was significantly higher. For a discussion of these studies and their implications, see Marius C. Vollberg and Mina Cikara (2018), 'The neuroscience of intergroup emotion', *Current Opinions in Psychology* 24, pp. 48–52.

11 Jay J. Van Bavel, Dominic J. Packer and William A. Cunningham (2008), 'The neural substrates of in-group bias', *Psychological Science* 19(11), pp. 1131–9.

12 William Graham Sumner, *Folkways: A study of the sociological importance of usages, manners, customs, mores, and morals* (Ginn, 1906), p. 13.

13 Given what we know about in-group out-group prejudice and the historical rivalry between Manchester United and Liverpool, we might have expected the participants to discriminate more against the jogger in the Liverpool shirt than in the unbranded shirt, to help him even less often. But on this occasion at least, favouring their own team was more important than derogating their rivals.

14 Mark Levine et al. (2005), 'Identity and emergency intervention: how social group membership and inclusiveness of group boundaries shape helping behavior', *Personality and Social Psychology Bulletin* 31(4), pp. 443–53.

15 *Human Groups and Social Categories*, pp. 1/7.

16 Marilynn Brewer and Donald Campbell, *Ethnocentrism and Intergroup Attitudes: East African evidence* (Sage, 1976).

17 Marilynn Brewer, 'Optimal distinctiveness theory: its history and development', in Paul Van Lange, Arie Kruglanski and Tory Higgins, eds, *Handbook of Theories of Social Psychology* (Sage, 2011), p. 83.

18 The role of cooperation in human evolution is a hotly disputed subject. For a guide to the latest thinking, see this special issue of *Nature Human Behaviour*, published on 9 July 2018: https://www. nature.com/collections/gvmywthghh.

19 Marilynn Brewer is also known for developing 'optimal

distinctiveness theory' as an alternative way of explaining how people identify with groups. ODT states that humans are characterized by two opposing needs – to belong to a group (to fit in), and to feel sufficiently distinctive (to stand out). Our social identities are determined by how we balance these two needs. We are uncomfortable both in large collectives and in isolation, and we strive to join groups that allow us to avoid both these conditions. This attempt to explain group identity in terms of individual cognitive processes (a person's need for distinctiveness) has been criticised by proponents of Tajfel and Turner's social identity perspective, which argues that social identities are independent of personal identities. The debate represents an ongoing tension between the American approach to social psychology (the individual defines the collective) and the European approach (social identities define the individual).

20   You can read more about her thinking on when in-group love leads to out-group hate in Marilynn Brewer (1999), 'The psychology of prejudice: ingroup love or outgroup hate?', *Journal of Social Issues* 55(3), pp. 429–44.

21   As recounted by Shankly on Granada TV's afternoon chat show *Live at Two*, 20 May 1981.

22   Nick Hornby, *Fever Pitch* (Victor Gollancz, 1992), pp. 186–7.

23   Toby Miller and Alec McHoul explore the use of the categorized we in their book *Popular Culture and Everyday Life* (Sage, 1998), ch. 3. For a full account of how the social identity perspective applies to sport, see Alexander Haslam, Katrien Fransen and Filip Boen, *The New Psychology of Sport and Exercise: The social identity approach* (Sage, 2020).

24   Martha Newson et al. (2020), 'Devoted fans release more cortisol when watching live soccer matches', *Stress and Health* 36(2), pp. 220–7. This study replicated a previous one by Leander van der Meij at the 2010 World Cup: Leander van der Meij et al. (2012), 'Testosterone and cortisol release among Spanish soccer fans watching the 2010 world cup final', *PLOS One* 7(4): e34814. Van der Meij found increased levels of both cortisol and testosterone, a

hormone released during challenging situations when a person's social status is threatened.

25 In Martha Newson, Michael Buhrmester and Harvey Whitehouse (2016), 'Explaining lifelong loyalty: the role of identity fusion and self-shaping group events', *PLOS One* 11(8): e0160427. Newson's other papers on this subject can be accessed at https://www.marthanewson.com/publications.

26 Daniel Wann et al. (2011), 'What would you do for a championship: willingness to consider acts of desperation among major league baseball fans', in Bruce Geranto, ed., *Sport Psychology* (Nova, 2011), pp. 161–73.

27 Robert Cialdini et al. (1976), 'Basking in reflected glory: three (football) field studies', *Journal of Personality and Social Psychology* 34(3), pp. 366–75.

28 There's also BIRFing, or basking in reflected failure, which allows fans to maintain loyalty and camaraderie even when their team is losing; and CORSing, or cutting off reflected success, practised by fans of successful teams who disapprove of the way the team is being run or what it stands for. See Richard Campbell, Damon Aiken and Aubrey Kent (2004), 'Beyond BIRGing and CORFing: continuing the exploration of fan behavior', *Sport Marketing Quarterly* 13, pp. 151–7.

29 *Fever Pitch*, p. 173.

30 Martha Newson, Michael Buhrmester and Harvey Whitehouse (2021), 'United in defeat: shared suffering and group bonding among football fans', *Managing Sport and Leisure*, https://www.tandfonline.com/doi/full/10.1080/23750472.2020.1866650. In a subsequent study, Newson's team has found that fans experience a greater sense of belonging and 'psychological synchrony' if they attend games in person, rather than watching remotely on a screen in small groups: Gabriela Baranowski-Pinto et al. (2022), 'Being in a crowd bonds people via physiological synchrony', *Nature Scientific Reports* 12:613, https://doi.org/10.1038/s41598-021-04548-2.

31 Gozde Ikizer (2014), 'Factors related to psychological resilience among survivors of the earthquakes in Van, Turkey', PhD thesis,

Graduate School of Social Sciences, Middle East Technical University, Ankara.

32　Some of these details were previously published in Michael Bond, 'The secrets of extraordinary survivors', *BBC Future*, 14 August 2015, available here: https://www.bbc.com/future/article/20150813-the-secrets-of-extraordinary-survivors.

33　Stepan Jurajda and Tomas Jelinek (2019), 'Surviving Auschwitz with pre-existing social ties', CERGE-EI Working Paper Series no. 646.

34　See Dora Costa and Matthew Kahn (2007), 'Surviving Andersonville: the benefits of social networks in POW camps', *The American Economic Review* 97(4), pp. 1467–87.

35　Metin Basoglu et al. (1997), 'Psychological preparedness for trauma as a protective factor in survivors of torture', *Psychological Medicine* 27(6), pp. 1421–33.

36　Alexander Haslam et al. (2005), 'Taking the strain: social identity, social support, and the experience of stress', *British Journal of Social Psychology* 44, pp. 355–70.

37　James Rubin et al. (2005), 'Psychological and behavioural reactions to the bombings in London on 7 July 2005: cross sectional survey of a representative sample of Londoners', *British Medical Journal* 331:606.

38　The term 'social cure' was coined by the psychologists Alexander Haslam, Catherine Haslam and Jolanda Jetten. For an in-depth discussion, see Catherine Haslam, Jolanda Jetten, Tegan Cruwys, Genevieve Dingle and Alexander Haslam, *The New Psychology of Health: Unlocking the social cure* (Routledge, 2018).

39　Julianne Holt-Lunstad, Timothy Smith and Bradley Layton (2010), 'Social relationships and mortality risk: a meta-analytic review', *PLOS Medicine* 7(7): e1000316.

40　Tegan Cruwys et al. (2014), 'Depression and social identity: an integrative review', *Personality and Social Psychology Review* 18(3), pp. 215–38. Psychologists have found a 'more the merrier' effect with social identity and health: the more groups a person identifies with, the greater the impact on their health and self-esteem. The number of groups you identify with is more important for your health than the number of interpersonal ties within those groups (the quality of those ties is paramount). For more on multiple group memberships, see Jolanda Jetten et al. (2015), 'Having a lot of a good thing: multiple important group memberships as a source of self-esteem', *PLOS One* 10(5): e0124609.

41   In a lab experiment, the psychologist Jan Hausser showed that the presence of others can reduce a person's cortisol levels after a stressful task but only if they perceive them as part of their in-group (i.e., if they share a social identity). Jan Hausser et al. (2012), '"We" are not stressed: social identity in groups buffers neuroendocrine stress reactions', *Journal of Experimental Social Psychology* 48, pp. 973–7.

42   For more details on Daniel Wann's research, see Daniel Wann and Jeffrey James, *Sports Fans: The psychology and social impact of fandom*, second edition (Taylor and Francis, 2019).

43   Patricia Obst, Lucy Zinkiewicz and Sandy Smith (2002), 'Sense of community in science fiction fandom, part 2: comparing neighbourhood and interest group sense of community', *Journal of Community Psychology* 30(1), pp. 105–17. This result was replicated in Daniel Chadborn, Patrick Edwards and Stephen Reysen (2016), 'Reexamining differences between fandom and local sense of community', *Psychology of Popular Media Culture* 7(3), pp. 241–9.

44   *The Posters Came from the Walls*, directed by Jeremy Deller and Nicholas Abrahams (1988).

45   Henry Jenkins (1988), '*Star Trek* rerun, reread, rewritten: fan writing as textual poaching', *Critical Studies in Mass Communication* 5(2), p. 87.

46   Bri Mattia (2018), 'Rainbow direction and fan-based citizenship performance', *Transformative Works and Cultures* 28, special 10th anniversary issue, available at http://dx.doi.org/10.3983/twc.2018.1414.

47   Available at https://catapult.co/stories/french-cartoon-led-to-fandom-and-friendship-miraculous-ladybug-loneliness-priyanka-bose.

CHAPTER 3: FICTIONAL FRIENDS

1   Details from Richard Lancelyn Green, ed., *Letters to Sherlock Holmes: A selection of the most interesting and entertaining of the letters written to the world's most famous detective* (Penguin, 1985). For more on Sherlock Holmes fan letters, see Tom Ue and Jonathan Cranfield, eds, *Fan Phenomena: Sherlock Holmes* (Intellect Books, 2014), pp. 70–2.

2   From the collection of the Sherlock Holmes Museum, London, 2016. Sherlock Holmes inspires a huge amount of fan activity around the world, with hundreds of clubs and societies dedicated to his adventures, and multiple television, film, radio and theatrical adaptations of the original works.

3   Donald Horton and Richard Wohl (1956), 'Mass communication and para-social interaction', *Psychiatry* 19(3), pp. 215–29.

4   See Tilo Hartmann, 'Parasocial interaction, parasocial relationships, and well-being', in Leonard Reinecke and Mary Beth Oliver, eds, *The Routledge Handbook of Media Use and Well-Being* (Routledge, 2017); and Randi Shedlosky-Shoemaker, Kristi Costabile and Robert Arkin (2014), 'Self-expansion through fictional characters', *Self and Identity* 13(5), pp. 556–78.

5   Donald Horton and Richard Wohl (1956).

6   Jonathan Cohen (2004), 'Parasocial break-up from favorite television characters: the role of attachment styles and relationship intensity', *Journal of Social and Personal Relationships* 21(2), pp. 187–202.

7   Jonathan Cohen (2004).

8   Wendi Gardner, Cynthia Pickett and Megan Knowles, 'Social snacking and shielding: using social symbols, selves, and surrogates in the service of belonging needs', in Kipling Williams, Joseph Forgas and William von Hippel, eds, *The Social Outcast: Ostracism, social exclusion, rejection, and bullying* (Psychology Press, 2005), pp. 227–41.

Meisam Vahedi at the University of Houston has found that religious people can achieve the same effect by attending to prayer objects such as beads and rosaries. For them God is an attachment figure, and contemplating the divine can help protect against the psychological impact of social rejection. Meisam Vahedi (2019), 'Prayer objects provide the experience of belonging', unpublished thesis. Abstract available at https://uh-ir.tdl.org/handle/10657/5350.

9   Why people should gain so much from fictive relationships is something of a mystery. How can it be? One possibility is that they don't perceive them as fictive at all. In 2008, Knowles and a colleague questioned two hundred undergraduates about their engagement with various television series, including popular sitcoms such as *Friends*, *Sex and the City* and *The Office* and dramas such as *Grey's Anatomy* and *24*. The researchers wanted to know how the students related to the characters, emotionally and intellectually. The most striking finding was that they treated their favourites (Phoebe in *Friends*, say) as more 'real' than the others (stand down Rachel, Monica, Chandler, Ross and Joey). They thought of them as actual people, ascribing them complex human emotional and cognitive traits. Wendi Gardner and Megan Knowles (2008), 'Love makes you real: favorite television characters are perceived as "real" in a social facilitation paradigm', *Social Cognition* 26(2), pp. 156–68.

10   Megan Knowles and Wendi Gardner (2012), '"I'll be there for you . . ." Favorite television characters as social surrogates', unpublished study.

    Social surrogates have also been found to help people with a history of trauma feel more socially connected. Paradoxically, trauma victims who have symptoms of post-traumatic stress disorder actually feel worse when they use social surrogates. These findings are published in Shira Gabriel et al. (2017), 'Social surrogate use in those exposed to trauma: I get by with a little help from my (fictional) friends', *Journal of Social and Clinical Psychology* 36(1), pp. 41–63.

11   Jaye Derrick, Shira Gabriel and Kurt Hugenberg (2009), 'Social surrogacy: how favored television programs provide the experience of belonging', *Journal of Experimental Social Psychology* 45, pp. 352–62.

12   Maggie Britton et al. (2020), 'Social surrogacy moderates the relationship between perceived partner responsiveness and smoking outcomes', poster presentation, University of Houston.

13   Inevitably, we don't always relate to the same character in the same way. Some of this difference may be due to culture. In 2011 a study of Mexican and German Harry Potter fans found that each interpreted the character through their own cultural lens. Mexican fans, whose culture is strongly collectivist, perceived the character to be more sociable than did German fans, whose culture is more individualistic. Hannah Schmid and Christoph Klimmt (2011), 'A magically nice guy: parasocial relationships with Harry Potter across different cultures', *The International Communication Gazette* 73(3), pp. 252–69.
It's well established that culture, as well as knowledge, experience and other influences, shapes how we interpret or remember stories. One of the first to demonstrate this was the early twentieth-century social psychologist Frederic Bartlett. When he asked a group of English students to re-tell a native American fairy tale, they altered it so that it fitted better with their own cultural background and attitudes. Frederic Bartlett, *Remembering: A study in experimental and social psychology* (Cambridge University Press, 1932).

14   For a neuroscientific explanation of how reading fiction might allow the brain to simulate hypothetical scenes, see Diana Tamir et al. (2016), 'Reading fiction and reading minds: the role of simulation in the default network', *Social Cognitive and Affective Neuroscience* 11(2), pp. 215–24.

15   For an up-to-date exploration of the psychology of people's relationships with fictional characters, see the collection of essays in Karen Shackleford, ed., *Real Characters: The psychology of parasocial relationships with media characters* (Fielding University Press, 2020).

16   Although the tradition of cosplay started in the US in the 1960s, the term 'cosplay' was coined by Japanese games designer Takahashi Nobuyuki in the 1980s.

17 Henry Jenkins (2012), 'Superpowered fans: the many worlds of
San Diego's Comic-Con', *Boom: A Journal of California* 2(2), pp. 22–36.

18 The tendency for some people to be drawn to the darker aspects
of themselves is explored in Rebecca Krause and Derek Rucker
(2020), 'Can good be bad? The attraction of a darker self',
Psychological Science 31(5), pp. 518–30.

19 Robin Rosenberg and Andrea Letamendi (2013), 'Expressions of
fandom: findings from a psychological survey of cosplay and
costume wear', *Intensities: The Journal of Cult Media* 5, pp. 9–18.

20 Robin Rosenberg and Andrea Letamendi (2018), 'Personality,
behavioral, and social heterogeneity within the cosplay
community', *Transformative Works and Cultures* 28, special 10th
anniversary issue, available at http://dx.doi.org/10.3983/
twc.2018.1535.

21 IARP has published dozens of peer-reviewed articles, book chapters
and conference papers, all of which are available on its website:
https://furscience.com. Much of the data on furries in this chapter
comes from IARP.

22 See Courtney Plante et al. (2018), 'Letters from Equestria: prosocial
media, helping, and empathy in fans of *My Little Pony*',
Communication and Culture Online 9, pp. 206–20. For more on this
and other findings, see Patrick Edwards et al., *Meet the Bronies: The
psychology of the adult* My Little Pony *fandom* (McFarland, 2019).
Further publications available on the website of the Brony
Research Project: https://sites.google.com/view/
bronystudyresearch/home.

23 This reflects a historical debate within psychology between
personality researchers, who study individual traits, and social
psychologists, who study how people behave in social contexts.
Personality researchers (largely based in the US) tend to believe
that personality is stable across the lifespan and across situations,
whereas social psychologists (largely based in Europe) argue that
personality is fluid and depending on which of someone's identities
is most pronounced or 'salient' at the time.

24 Stephen Reysen et al. (2015), 'A social identity perspective of

personality differences between fan and non-fan identities', *World Journal of Social Science Research* 2(1), pp. 91–103.

25 *Fifty Shades of Grey* (Vintage, 2011) started out as a fan fiction story titled *Masters of the Universe*, based on the television drama *Twilight*; *Wide Sargasso Sea* (André Deutsch / W. W. Norton, 1966) was a feminist, anti-colonial response to Charlotte Brontë's *Jane Eyre*.

26 These examples come via David Brewer, *The Afterlife of Character, 1726–1825* (University of Pennsylvania Press, 2005).

27 For further detail see Ann McClellan, *Sherlock's World: Fan fiction and the reimagining of BBC's* Sherlock (University of Iowa Press, 2018); and Tom Ue and Jonathan Cranfield, eds, *Fan Phenomena: Sherlock Holmes* (Intellect Books, 2014).

28 https://archiveofourown.org.

29 'Am I the asshole for dueling my friend?', by earsXfeet6669, published on Archive of Our Own.

30 'A house full of ghosts', by opheliasnettles, published on Archive of Our Own.

31 For more on Harry Potter fan fiction, see Catherine Tosenberger (2008), 'Homosexuality at the online Hogwarts: Harry Potter slash fanfiction', *Children's Literature* 36, pp. 185–207.

32 From an analysis of 2013 census data from Archive of Our Own, available here: https://archiveofourown.org/works/16988199?view_full_work=true. A more recent study of Harry Potter fans on Archive of Our Own, which estimated that between 50 and 75 per cent identified as female, suggests that the demographics of highly engaged fandoms may be changing: Jennifer Duggan (2020), 'Who writes Harry Potter fan fiction? Passionate detachment, "zooming out," and fan fiction paratexts on AO3', *Transformative Works and Cultures* 34, special 10th anniversary issue, available at https://journal.transformativeworks.org/index.php/twc/article/view/1863/2599.

33 For a more in-depth analysis of this issue, see Elizabeth Minkel, 'Why it doesn't matter what Benedict Cumberbatch thinks of Sherlock fan fiction', *New Statesman*, 17 October 2014. Available here: https://www.newstatesman.com/culture/2014/10/

why-it-doesn-t-matter-what-benedict-cumberbatch-thinks-sherlock-fan-fiction.

34 In Archive of Our Own's 2013 census, less than 30 per cent of respondents identified as heterosexual, and only 4 per cent as male: https://archiveofourown.org/works/16988199?view_full_work=true. In Jennifer Duggan's (2020) analysis of Harry Potter fans, 35 per cent described themselves as queer or gay and 29 per cent as pan- or bisexual.

35 From Lev Grossman's forward to *Fic: Why fanfiction is taking over the world*, by Anne Jamison (Smart Pop / BenBella Books, 2013).

36 Available on Archive of Our Own at https://archiveofourown.org/works/10655448/chapters/23579739.

37 Available on Archive of Our Own at https://archiveofourown.org/works/5870761/chapters/13552171.

38 Available on Archive of Our Own at https://archiveofourown.org/works/121330.

39 For further discussion of the nature of fan fiction writers' parasocial relationships, including acknowledgement of the lack of research on the subject, see Jennifer Barnes (2015), 'Fanfiction as imaginary play: what fan-written stories can tell us about the cognitive science of fiction', *Poetics* 48, pp. 69–82.

40 https://improbablepress.co.uk.

41 Atlin Merrick's Sherlock fiction can be read on Archive of Our Own here: https://archiveofourown.org/works/875175/chapters/1681916. Her books are *The Night They Met* (Clan Destine Press, 2015); and *The Day They Met* (MX Publishing, 2015), under the pen name Wendy C. Fries.

CHAPTER 4: REACH FOR THE STARS

1 Homer, *The Iliad*, translated by Robert Fagles (Penguin, 1991): 22.346.

2 For more on biographical details of classical heroes see Seth Schein, *The Mortal Hero: An introduction to Homer's Iliad* (University of California Press, 1985); and Gregory Nagy, *The Ancient Greek Hero in 24 Hours* (Belknap Press, 2013).

3   Bandura later renamed his theory 'social cognitive theory'. For a full explanation see Albert Bandura, *Social Foundations of Thought and Action: A social cognitive theory* (Prentice-Hall, 1986).

4   The role of personality in people's attraction to a public figure is disputed by some psychologists, though there is evidence for it. For example, Gayle Stever (1991), 'Imaginary social relationships and personality correlates: the case of Michael Jackson and his fans', *Journal of Psychological Type* 21, pp. 68–76; and David Greenberg et al. (2020), 'The self-congruity effect of music', *Journal of Personality and Social Psychology* 121(1), pp. 137–50.

5   For further explanation of Stever's methodology, see Gayle Stever (2019), 'Fan studies in psychology: a road less traveled', *Transformative Works and Cultures* 30, available at https://doi.org/10.3983/twc.2019.1641.

6   Gayle Stever (1991).

7   For more on how simulating others can change aspects of the self, see Jaye Derrick, Shira Gabriel and Brooke Tippin (2008), 'Parasocial relationships and self-discrepancies: faux relationships have benefits for low self-esteem individuals', *Personal Relationships* 15, pp. 261–280; and Meghan Meyer, Zidong Zhao and Diana Tamir (2019), 'Simulating other people changes the self', *Journal of Experimental Psychology: General* 148(11), pp. 1898–913.

8   Riva Tukachinsky and Sybilla Dorros (2018), 'Parasocial romantic relationships, romantic beliefs, and relationship outcomes in US adolescents: rehearsing love or setting oneself up to fail?', *Journal of Children and Media* 12(3), pp. 329–45. Tukachinsky has found that parasocial romantic relationships, where a person feels a loving or sexual attraction to a celebrity or character, are surprisingly common: out of a sample of 566 people, 60 per cent reported that they had at least one. For more on her work on this subject, see Riva Tukachinsky Forster, *Parasocial Romantic Relationships: Falling in love with media figures* (Lexington, 2021).

9   This interviewee preferred to remain anonymous.

10 For more about the social psychology of leadership and followership, see Alexander Haslam and Stephen Reicher (2016),

'Rethinking the psychology of leadership: from personal identity to social identity', *Daedalus, the Journal of the American Academy of Arts and Sciences* 145(3), pp. 21–34; and Alexander Haslam, Stephen Reicher and Michael Platow, *The New Psychology of Leadership: Identity, influence and power* (Psychology Press, 2011).

11 David Foster Wallace, 'Roger Federer as religious experience', *New York Times*, 20 August 2006. Available here: https://www.nytimes.com/2006/08/20/sports/playmagazine/20federer.html.

12 These details are taken from Margaret Farrand Thorpe, *America at the Movies* (Yale University Press, 1939), pp. 96–7. In Chapter 5, we'll explore why celebrities' personal objects are so revered by their fans.

13 Their research material, from which the quotes in this section are taken, was published in Fred and Judy Vermorel, *Starlust: The secret life of fans* (W. H. Allen, 1985).

14 Fred and Judy Vermorel, *Starlust: The secret life of fans* (W. H. Allen, 1985), afterword.

15 In Lisa Lewis, ed., *The Adoring Audience: Fan culture and popular media* (Routledge, 1992), p. 128.

16 Data via email from Graceland: The Home of Elvis Presley, www.graceland.com.

17 From Benson Fraser and William Brown (2002), 'Media, celebrities and social influence: identification with Elvis Presley', *Mass Communication and Society* 5(2), pp. 183–206.

18 Details of Ben Thompson's Elvis shows can be found on his website: https://www.benthompsonaselvis.com.

19 For further analysis of Elvis re-enactors and fans, see Benson Fraser and William Brown (2002); also Mark Duffett (1998), 'Understanding Elvis: Presley, power and performance', unpublished PhD thesis, University of Wales, ch. 7, available at https://ethos.bl.uk/OrderDetails.do?uin=uk.bl.ethos.343561.

20 The Beatles Sessions can be booked at https://thebeatlessessions.nl. Unlike the Beatles, they are a five-piece, to ensure that they can perform the songs live as they were recorded.

21 In an article for the *Daily Mirror*.

22 Don Short became good friends with the Beatles and accompanied

them on all their tours, eventually breaking the story of their split on 9 April 1970. For an account of his extraordinary career, in which in addition to the Beatles he interviewed and befriended numerous celebrities from Elvis to Muhammad Ali, see his book *The Beatles and Beyond: The memoirs of Don Short* (Wymer Publishing, 2020).

23 Paul Johnson, 'The menace of Beatlism', *New Statesman*, February 1964, available here: https://www.newstatesman.com/culture/2014/08/archive-menace-beatlism. Not everyone in the establishment saw it this way. In the same article, Johnson criticized government minister William Deedes for saying that the Beatles 'herald a cultural movement among the young which may become part of the history of our time . . . For those with eyes to see it, something important and heartening is happening here.'

24 Barbara Ehrenreich, Elizabeth Hess and Gloria Jacobs, 'Beatlemania: girls just want to have fun', in Lisa Lewis, ed., *The Adoring Audience: Fan culture and popular media* (Routledge, 1992), pp. 103–4.

25 Jonathan Heaf, 'This One Direction interview got us death threats', British *GQ*, September 2013, available here: https://www.gq-magazine.co.uk/article/one-direction-gq-covers-interview.

26 Mark Duffett, 'I scream therefore I fan? Music audiences and affective citizenship', in Jonathan Gray, Cornell Sandvoss and Lee Harrington, eds, *Fandom: Identities and communities in a mediated world*, 2nd edition (NYU Press, 2017), pp. 143–56.

27 Kaitlyn Tiffany, *Everything I Need I Get From You: How fangirls created the internet as we know it* (MCD x FSG Originals, 2022), p. 48.

28 *The Beatles Anthology* television documentary series, 1995, disc 2, episode 4.

29 Cameron Crowe, 'Harry Styles' new direction', *Rolling Stone*, 18 April 2017, available here: https://www.rollingstone.com/feature/harry-styles-new-direction-119432/.

30 Dave Garroway as told to Joe Alex Morris, 'I lead a goofy life', *The Saturday Evening Post*, 11 February 1956, p. 62.

31 In Kaitlyn Tiffany, 'I love you Jake Gyllenhaal', *The Verge*,

3 November 2017, available here: https://www.theverge.
com/2017/11/3/16576850/jake-gyllenhaal-newsletter-fandom-
fans-essay

32 Kaitlyn Tiffany, 'Does Jake Gyllenhaal know I'm in this room?',
Medium, 22 September 2018, available here: https://medium.com/@
kait.tiffany/does-jake-gyllenhaal-know-im-in-this-room-d7de57d3fec2.

33 Fred and Judy Vermorel, *Starlust: The secret life of fans* (W. H. Allen,
1985).

34 *Starlust.*

35 Nancy Baym, *Playing to the Crowd: Musicians, audiences, and the
intimate work of connection* (New York University Press, 2018).

36 More details in Bradley Bond (2016), 'Following your "friend":
social media and the strength of adolescents' parasocial
relationships with media personae', *Cyberpsychology, Behavior, and
Social Networking* 19(11), pp. 656–60.

37 Originally called the Celebrity Worship Scale.

38 Lynn McCutcheon, Rense Lange and James Houran (2002),
'Conceptualization and measurement of celebrity worship', *British
Journal of Psychology* 93, pp. 67–87; and John Maltby et al. (2002),
'Thou shalt worship no other gods – unless they are celebrities: the
relationship between celebrity worship and religious orientation',
Personality and Individual Differences 32, pp. 1157–72.

39 John Maltby et al. (2006), 'Extreme celebrity worship, fantasy
proneness and dissociation: developing the measurement and
understanding of celebrity worship within a clinical personality
context', *Personality and Individual Differences* 40, pp. 273-83; and
Agnes Zsila, Lynn McCutcheon and Zsolt Demetrovics (2018), 'The
association of celebrity worship with problematic internet use,
maladaptive daydreaming, and desire for fame', *Journal of Behavioral
Addictions* 7(3), pp. 654–64.

40 There is evidence that people with certain personality traits, such
as neuroticism, may be more prone to this behaviour. See John
Maltby, Lynn McCutcheon and Robert Lowinger (2011), 'Brief
report: celebrity worshipers and the five-factor model of
personality', *North American Journal of Psychology* 13(2), pp. 343–8.

41 Louis Schlesinger (2006), 'Celebrity stalking, homicide, and suicide', *International Journal of Offender Therapy and Comparative Criminology* 50(1), pp. 39–46.

42 Lindsay Baker, 'Norse code', *Guardian Weekend*, 27 September 1997.

43 Lily Allen, *My Thoughts Exactly* (Blink Publishing, 2018), p. 300.

44 You can listen to Lizzyspit's music at https://soundcloud.com/lizzyspit.

CHAPTER 5: SOMETHING ABOUT JANE

1 *Northanger Abbey* and *Persuasion*.

2 Jane Austen, *Northanger Abbey* (Little, Brown, 1903), p. 90.

3 The Georgian era of British history lasted from 1714 to around 1837; the Regency, during which Jane Austen lived, covers the last part of that era, from 1795, when George IV assumed the role of prince regent during the illness of his father George III.

4 The term was coined by the literary scholar George Saintsbury in his introduction to an 1894 edition of *Pride and Prejudice*. Austen's fans in that era were also known as Austenites.

5 The cause of Jane Austen's death has been much disputed. The latest diagnosis of systemic lupus erythematosus, by emeritus consultants Michael Saunders and Elizabeth Graham at St Thomas' Hospital in London, comes from a detailed review of the medical information in her surviving letters. Michael Saunders and Elizabeth Graham (2021), '"Black and white and every wrong colour": the medical history of Jane Austen and the possibility of systemic lupus erythematosus', *Lupus* 30(4), pp. 549–53.

6 James Edward Austen-Leigh, *A Memoir of Jane Austen*, 2nd edition (Richard Bentley, 1871).

7 *A Memoir of Jane Austen*, pp. 2, 87.

8 Leslie Stephen (1876), 'Humour', *Cornhill Magazine* xxxiii, pp. 318–26.

9 Reginald Farrer (1917), 'Jane Austen – ob. July 18, 1817', *The Quarterly Review* 228(452), pp. 1–30.

10 Kipling's story was published in several magazines in May 1924 and is available here: http://www.telelib.com/authors/K/KiplingRudyard/prose/DebtsandCredits/janeites.html.

11 http://laughingwithlizzie.blogspot.com.

12 Sophie Andrews, *Be More Jane: Bring out your inner Austen to meet life's challenges* (Cico Books, 2019).

13 Deborah Yaffe, *Among the Janeites: A journey through the world of Jane Austen fandom* (Mariner Books, 2013), pp. 225–6.

14 D. W. Harding (1939), 'Regulated hatred: an aspect of the work of Jane Austen', in Monica Lawlor, ed., *Regulated Hatred and Other Essays on Jane Austen* (Bloomsbury, 1998).

15 Jane Austen, *Pride and Prejudice* (Purnell, 1977), p. 13.

16 Austen fans who enjoy her social criticism will find much to savour in her 'Juvenilia', the collection of plays, short stories and musings that she wrote between the ages of twelve and sixteen. Generally read only by the most committed Janeites, they contain some of her most spirited social commentary.

17 Helen Fielding, *Bridget Jones's Diary* (Picador, 1996).

18 Seth Grahame-Smith, *Pride and Prejudice and Zombies* (Quirk, 2009).

19 Seth Grahame-Smith quoted in Liz Goodwin, 'Monsters vs. Jane Austen', *The Daily Beast*, 31 March 2009, available at http://www.thedailybeast.com/articles/2009/03/31/monsters-vs-jane-austen.html.

20 https://austenprose.com/.

21 Abigail Reynolds, *What Would Mr Darcy Do?* (Sourcebooks, 2011).

22 Brenda J. Webb, *Mr Darcy's Forbidden Love* (CreateSpace, 2012).

23 Amanda Grange, *Mr Darcy, Vampyre* (Sourcebooks, 2009).

24 Caitlin Marie Carrington, *Snowbound with Darcy* (Caitlin Marie Carrington, 2018).

25 Enid Wilson, *My Darcy Vibrates . . .* (Steamy D, 2011).

26 Sarah Roberts et al. (2010), 'Darcin: a male pheromone that stimulates female memory and sexual attraction to an individual male's odour', *BMC Biology* 8, article 75.

27 Sourced from Holly Luetkenhaus and Zoe Weinstein, *Austentatious: The evolving world of Jane Austen fans* (University of Iowa Press,

2019), ch. 5. This work of fan fiction was published on Archive of Our Own but is no longer available.

28 For further discussions on race and diversity in Austen's novels, see 'Beyond the bit of ivory', a special edition of *Persuasions* 41(2), summer 2021, available at https://jasna.org/publications-2/persuasions-online/volume-41-no-2.

29 Constance Hill, *Jane Austen: Her homes and her friends* (John Lane, 1902), p. 14.

30 Francis Darwin, *Rustic Sounds and Other Studies in Literature and Natural History* (John Murray, 1917), pp. 76–7. This reference and the reference to Lord Tennyson are sourced from Peter Graham (2004), 'Why Lyme Regis?', *Persuasions* 26, pp. 27–40.

31 For more details of Ibthorpe and other houses associated with Jane Austen, see Nigel Nicolson, *The World of Jane Austen* (Weidenfeld & Nicolson, 1991).

32 The Austen-era wallpaper was printed for the museum by Bruce Fine Papers of North Hykeham, Lincolnshire (http://www.brucefinepapers.com) and supplied by Hamilton Weston Wallpapers of London (https://hamiltonweston.com).

33 Nicola Watson, 'Austen at her desk', The Literary Tourist blog, 5 February 2014, http://www.open.ac.uk/blogs/literarytourist/?p=89. See also Nicola Watson, *The Literary Tourist: Readers and places in Romantic and Victorian Britain* (Palgrave Macmillan, 2006).

34 Constance Hill, *Jane Austen*, p. 172. For a good analysis of how lovers of Austen have interpreted her legacy, see Claudia Johnson, *Jane Austen's Cults and Cultures* (University of Chicago Press, 2012).

35 George Newman and Paul Bloom (2014), 'Physical contact influences how much people pay at celebrity auctions', *PNAS* 111(10), pp. 3705–8. The researchers found that the contagion effect may not work in the same way with celebrities who are perceived as being morally negative; in this case, objects with a perceived physical connection to the disgraced financier Bernard Madoff did not sell at a premium. This fails to explain why there is such a strong market for objects associated with serial killers and other criminals, as we'll see in this book's final chapter.

For more insight into psychological contagion, see Newman and Bloom's earlier paper, George Newman, Gil Diesendruck and Paul Bloom (2011), 'Celebrity contagion and the value of objects', *Journal of Consumer Research* 38(2), pp. 215–28; also Kristan Marchak and Geoffrey Hall (2017), 'Transforming celebrity objects: implications for an account of psychological contagion', *Journal of Cognition and Culture* 17, pp. 51–72.

CHAPTER 6: ANIMAL MINDS

1   The word 'therianthropy' is derived from the Greek words for beast and human. Therian is an abbreviated form of 'therianthrope'.

2   One unpublished survey by a social psychologist in Alabama, based only on that state, estimated that therians make up 0.03 per cent of the general population, or 3 in 10,000. From interview with Wolf VanZandt, 4 August 2020.

3   All real names of therians in this chapter have been hidden to protect their identity.

4   In Japan the belief that you have been possessed by a fox is known as *kitsunetsuki*. It appears to be specific to the culture; some psychiatrists consider it a mental condition similar to lycanthropy.

5   For survey data on the prevalence of phantom limbs and other therianthropic experiences among a group of therians, see Courtney Plante, Stephen Reysen, Sharon Roberts and Kathleen Gerbasi, *Fur Science! A summary of five years of research from the International Anthropomorphic Research Project* (FurScience, 2016), p. 116. Further information about the IARP's research is available at https://furscience.com.

6   Ronald Melzack (1992), 'Phantom limbs', *Scientific American* 266(4), pp. 120–6. For further research on this subject, see Peter Halligan (2002), 'Phantom limbs: the body in mind', *Cognitive Neuropsychiatry* 7(3), pp. 251–68; and Peter Brugger (2000), 'Beyond re-membering: phantom sensations of congenitally absent limbs', *PNAS* 97(11), pp. 6167–72.

7   Devin Proctor (2019), 'On Being Non-Human: Otherkin Identification and Virtual Space', graduate dissertation submitted to the Columbian College of Arts and Sciences, George Washington University.

8   Paul Keck et al. (1988), 'Lycanthropy: alive and well in the twentieth century', *Psychological Medicine* 18(1), pp. 113–20.

9   Helen Thomson, *Unthinkable: An Extraordinary Journey through the World's Strangest Brains* (John Murray, 2018), ch. 6.

10 Helen Clegg, Roz Collings and Elizabeth Roxburgh (2019), 'Therianthropy: wellbeing, schizotypy, and autism in individuals who self-identify as non-human', *Society and Animals* 27, pp. 403–26. In separate studies, Elizabeth Fein, a psychologist at Duquesne University, has found an incidence of autism among the furry fandom of between 5 and 15 per cent. Anecdotally, she believes the incidence among therians (some of whom are also furries) may be comparable, though she can't be sure without collecting more data.

11 For more on the healthy expression of schizotypal traits, see Christine Mohr and Gordon Claridge (2015), 'Schizotypy – do not worry, it is not all worrisome', *Schizophrenia Bulletin* 41(2), pp. S436–S443.

12 Gerbasi and Fein present a useful analysis of the work they have conducted together with the therian community in Kathleen Gerbasi and Elizabeth Fein, 'Furries, therians and otherkin, oh my! What do all those words mean anyway?', in Thurston Howl, ed., *Furries Among Us 2: More essays on furries by furries* (Thurston Howl Publications, 2017), pp. 162–76.

13 The New King James version, chapter 1, verse 28.

14 In René Descartes, *Discourse on the Method* (1637).

15 For those wishing to read more on the history and science of human–animal interactions, two good sources are Margo DeMello, *Animals and Society: An introduction to human–animal studies* (Columbia University Press, 2012); and Samantha Hurn, *Humans and Other Animals: Cross-cultural perspectives on human–animal interactives* (Pluto Press, 2012).

16 Quoted in Daniel Brinton (1894), 'Nagualism: a study in Native American folklore and history', read before the American Philosophical Society, 5 January 1894.

17 Some of the details from this paragraph are taken from John Kachuba, *Shapeshifters: A history* (Reaktion Books, 2019), an excellent source on the cultural history of shapeshifting folklore.

18 Thomas Thwaites, *Goat Man: How I Took a Holiday from Being Human* (Princeton Architectural Press, 2016), p. 169. Around the same time, Charles Foster, a lecturer in medical ethics, experimented with living like a badger, a fox, an otter, a deer and other animals, described in Charles Foster, *Being a Beast* (Profile Books, 2016).

19 From an interview with Thomas Thwaites published in the *Guardian*, 15 May 2016. Available here: https://www.theguardian.com/science/shortcuts/2016/may/15/no-kidding-what-learned-from-becoming-goatman.

20 This may have contributed to the high rates of post-traumatic stress disorder among Vietnam veterans. See Karestan Koenen et al. (2003), 'Risk factors for course of posttraumatic stress disorder among Vietnam veterans: a 14-year follow-up of American Legionnaires', *Journal of Consulting and Clinical Psychology* 71(6), pp. 980–6. Also Elisa Bolton (2002), 'The impact of homecoming reception on the adaptation of peacekeepers following deployment', *Military Psychology* 14, pp. 241–51.

21 The psychologist Helen Clegg suggests that therians who have theriotypes that are considered stereotypically positive – such as felines and canines, which are typically seen as majestic, cute, loyal, courageous and so on – may find it easier to adjust and feel more accepted by their wider community. 'Being an animal that is positively valued by society allows them to internally accept their therian status more,' she explains in an email. This would tally with previous psychological research showing that positive and negative stereotypes can have a big impact on people's well-being. Helen Clegg, Roz Collings and Elizabeth Roxburgh (2019), p. 421.

22 In a recent survey on one therian forum, around 35 per cent of respondents reported being sexually attracted to animals. Of those

35 per cent, most were attracted to animals of their own theriotype.

23 The idea that identifying with a disadvantaged group can improve psychological well-being is known in psychology as the 'rejection–identification model'. For further explanation, see Michael Schmitt and Nyla Branscombe, 'The meaning and consequences of perceived discrimination in disadvantaged and privileged social groups', in Wolfgang Stroebe and Miles Hewstone, eds, *European Review of Social Psychology* (John Wiley, 2002), ch. 6. Also relevant is Marilynn Brewer's optimal distinctiveness theory, described in Chapter 2, note 19.

Researchers have found a link between group stigmatization, identification and psychological well-being among various fan groups, including furries, bronies and fans of Japanese animé and manga. See Andrew Tague, Stephen Reysen and Courtney Plante (2020), 'Belongingness as a mediator of the relationship between felt stigma and identification in fans', *Journal of Social Psychology* 160(3), pp. 324–31.

CHAPTER 7: THROUGH THE BAD TIMES AND THE GOOD

1   https://www.imdb.com.

2   Julie Burchill, *Damaged Gods: Cults and heroes reappraised* (Century, 1986); quoted in Henry Jenkins, *Textual Poachers: Television fans and participatory culture* (Routledge, 2013), pp. 13–14.

3   For more on Mark Chapman and pathological models of fandom, see Mark Duffett, *Understanding Fandom: An introduction to the study of media fan culture* (Bloomsbury, 2013), ch. 4.

4   Based on papers obtained from the Metropolitan Police by David Clarke at Sheffield Hallam University, via a Freedom of Information request in 2005. More info at https://drdavidclarke.co.uk/2015/05/17/ufo-new-religious-movements-and-the-millennium/.

5   Laura Vroomen (2002), '"This Woman's Work": Kate Bush, female fans and practices of distinction', Ph.D. thesis, Centre for the Study of Women and Gender, University of Warwick.

6   In Fred and Judy Vermorel, *Starlust: The secret life of fans* (W. H. Allen, 1985).

7   In email correspondence.

8   Henry Jenkins (2012), 'Fan studies at the crossroads: an interview with Lynn Zubernis and Katherine Larsen (part two)', available at http://henryjenkins.org/blog/2012/09/fan-studies-at-the-crossroads-an-interview-with-lynn-zubernis-and-katherine-larsen-part-two.html. For more on this subject, see Elizabeth Cohen (2015), 'Sports fans and sci-fi fanatics: the social stigma of popular media fandom', *Psychology of Popular Media Culture* 6(3), pp. 193–207.

9   Lynn Zubernis's latest book is *There'll Be Peace When You Are Done: Actors and fans celebrate the legacy of Supernatural* (Smart Pop, 2020).

10   Casey Johnston, 'The death of the "gamers" and the women who "killed" them', *Ars Technica*, 29 August 2014. Available here: https://arstechnica.com/gaming/2014/08/the-death-of-the-gamers-and-the-women-who-killed-them.

11   For an analysis of the identity dynamics behind Gamergate and polarization in internet-based fandoms, see Hannah Abramson (2020), 'Haters, gatekeepers, and stans: the effects of social media on fandoms and the established order', *The Phoenix Papers* 4(2), pp. 119–30.

12   Josef Adalian et al., 'The 25 most devoted fan bases', *Vulture*, 15 October 2012. Available here: https://www.vulture.com/2012/10/25-most-devoted-fans.html.

13   Sarah Hughes, 'Interview – George R. R. Martin: "Game of Thrones finishing is freeing, I'm at my own pace"', *The Observer*, 18 August 2019. Available here: https://www.theguardian.com/books/2019/aug/18/george-rr-martin-interview-game-of-thrones-at-own-pace-now.

14   Darren Tak Lun Wong and Lefteris Patlamazoglou (2020), 'Bereavement and coping following the death of a personally significant popular musician', *Death Studies*, DOI: 10.1080/07481187.2020.1809031.

15   In author interview.

16   For example, Jimmy Sanderson and Pauline Cheong (2010), 'Tweeting prayers and communicating grief over Michael Jackson online', *Bulletin of Science, Technology and Society* 30(5), pp. 328–40.

This study found that following Jackson's death, fans moved through the five stages of Elisabeth Kübler-Ross's seminal model of grieving in their postings on Twitter, Facebook and TMZ.com.

17 Didier Courbet and Marie-Pierre Fourquet-Courbet (2014). 'When a celebrity dies . . . social identity, uses of social media, and the mourning process among fans: the case of Michael Jackson', *Celebrity Studies* 5(3), pp. 275–90.

18 From Twitter UK: https://twitter.com/TwitterUK/status/686504368456253440.

19 Shelly Tan, 'An illustrated guide to all 6,887 deaths in "Game of Thrones" ', *Washington Post*, 21 May 2019. Available here: https://www.washingtonpost.com/graphics/entertainment/game-of-thrones/.

20 Emory Daniel Jr. and David Westerman (2017), 'Valar morghulis (all parasocial men must die): having nonfictional responses to a fictional character', *Communication Research Reports* 34(2), pp. 143–52.

21 *Slate's* virtual Game of Thrones graveyard lives at http://www.slate.com/articles/arts/television/2014/04/game_of_thrones_deaths_mourn_dead_characters_at_their_virtual_graveyard.html.

22 Rosa Schiavone, Stijn Reijnders and Balázs Boross (2019), 'Losing an imagined friend: deriving meaning from fictional death in popular culture', *Participations: Journal of Audience and Reception Studies* 16(2), pp. 118–34.

23 These hedging strategies are known in psychology as CORFing – 'cutting off reflected failure' – a concept we covered briefly in Chapter 2. For further research into how fans deal with threats to their identity see Nola Agha and David Tyler (2017), 'An investigation of highly identified fans who bet against their favorite teams', *Sport Management Review* 20, pp. 296–308; Elizabeth Delia (2017), 'March madness: coping with fan identity threat', *Sport Management Review* 20, pp. 408–21; and Daniel Wann and Jeffrey James, *Sports Fans: The psychology and social impact of fandom*, second edition (Taylor & Francis, 2019), pp. 187–93.

24 Emily Nussbaum, 'Confessions of the human shield', in *I Like to Watch: Arguing my way through the TV revolution* (Random House, 2019), pp. 112–13.

25   www.MJJCommunity.com.

26   Joe Coscarelli, 'Michael Jackson fans are tenacious. "Leaving
      Neverland" has them poised for battle', *New York Times*, 4 March
      2019. Available here: https://www.nytimes.com/2019/03/04/arts/
      music/michael-jackson-leaving-neverland-fans.html.

27   See Joon Sung Lee, Dae Hee Kwak and Jessica Braunstein-Minkove
      (2016), 'Coping with athlete endorsers' immoral behavior: roles of
      athlete identification and moral emotion on moral reasoning
      strategies', *Journal of Sport Management* 30, pp. 176–91.

28   More information about the initiative is available at https://www.
      mjinnocent.com/.

29   'Jacco' was a Cockney slang term for monkeys that apparently
      derives from Jacco Macacco, the name of a famous fighting
      monkey that featured in monkey-baiting matches at the
      Westminster Pit in London in the 1820s.

30   In Paul Murray Kendall, *Richard the Third* (George Allen and
      Unwin, 1956), Appendix II, p. 420.

31   More by his own admission was writing from sources that were
      loyal to Richard III's rival and successor Henry VII.

32   Thomas More, *The History of King Richard III*, ed. Paul Kendall
      (The Folio Society, 1965), p. 35.

33   *The History of King Richard III*, p. 143.

34   William Shakespeare, *Richard III*, 1. 3. 246 (Cambridge University
      Press, 1954).

35   *Richard III*, 1. 1. 14–17.

36   *Richard III*, 1. 1. 19–23.

37   *Richard III*, 1. 1. 30–35.

38   Horace Walpole, *Historic Doubts on the Life and Reign of King Richard
      III*, ed. Paul Kendall (The Folio Society, 1965), p. 231.

39   *Historic Doubts on the Life and Reign of King Richard III*, p. 220.

40   Jane Austen, *The History of England* in her 'Juvenilia' (Cambridge
      University Press, 2006).

41   In Jeremy Potter, *Good King Richard? An account of Richard III and
      his reputation 1483–1983* (Constable, 1983), p. 258.

42   Published in *The Ricardian Bulletin*, September 2020.

43 For many members, their first introduction to this alternative view of Richard III is Paul Murray Kendall's *Richard the Third* and Josephine Tey's detective novel *The Daughter of Time* (Peter Davies, 1951).

44 The full version of this story, 'Well Met', is available at Archive of Our Own: https://archiveofourown.org/works/2238837. Two more of Harris's Ricardian fan fiction stories are published in *Grant Me the Carving of My Name: A collection of short stories inspired by Richard III*, ed. Alex Marchant (Marchant Ventures, 2018). For further details about her writing and published works, see https://narrellemharris.com.

45 More details in Anne Sutton and P. W. Hammond, *The Coronation of Richard III: the Extant Documents* (Alan Sutton, 1983).

46 The 'Voice for Richard' project is run by Yvonne Morley-Chisholm: www.yourvoicebox.co.uk.

47 He is occasionally mentioned in Parliament. The 1980 Broadcasting Bill, which originally allowed members of the public to sue producers for libel on behalf of the dead, was amended after it was pointed out that Ricardians would take full advantage of this whenever Shakespeare's *Richard III* was broadcast. The amendment, known as 'the Richard III clause', allowed complaints on behalf of the dead only for programmes broadcast within five years of their death. These details come from *Good King Richard?*, pp. 263–4.

48 Philippa Langley and Michael Jones, *The King's Grave: The search for Richard III* (John Murray, 2013), pp. 212–16.

49 Channel 4, *Richard III: The King in the Car Park*, broadcast on 4 February 2013.

50 Langley is working on a television documentary about the Missing Princes project for broadcast in 2022. For more information about her research, see https://www.revealingrichardiii.com/langley.html.

CHAPTER 8: MONSTERS LIKE US

1   From transcript of the Columbine 'Basement Tapes', available at https://schoolshooters.info/sites/default/files/columbine_basement_tapes_1.0.pdf.

NOTES

2   Even those who agree with Harris and Klebold's disturbing view of the world are highly unlikely to do anything about it. Studies of terrorism show that only a tiny minority of people with radical ideas ever resort to violence. For this reason, trying to pre-empt a terrorist act by targeting radicalized thinking is not a particularly efficient strategy (it may also trigger a backlash among marginalized communities). For more on this disconnect between belief and action, see Clark McCarley and Sophia Moskalenko (2016), 'Understanding political radicalization: the two-pyramids model', *American Psychologist* 72(3), pp. 205–16; and Peter Neumann (2013), 'The trouble with radicalization', *International Affairs* 89(4), pp. 873–93.

3   Quoted in Andrew Rico (2015), 'Fans of Columbine shooters Eric Harris and Dylan Klebold', *Transformative Works and Cultures* 20, available at https://doi.org/10.3983/twc.2015.0671.

4   From Jenni Raitanen and Atte Oksanen (2018), 'Global online subculture surrounding school shootings', *American Behavioral Scientist* 62(2), pp. 195–209.

5   Sveinung Sandberg et al. (2014), 'Stories in action: the cultural influences of school shootings on the terrorist attacks in Norway', *Critical Studies on Terrorism* 7(2), pp. 277–96.

6   For example, see Nina Lindberg et al. (2012), 'Adolescents expressing school massacre threats online: something to be extremely worried about?', *Child and Adolescent Psychiatry and Mental Health* 6:39.

7   Extracts taken from Jenni Raitanen, Sveinung Sandberg and Atte Oksanen (2019), 'The bullying–school shooting nexus: bridging master narratives of mass violence with personal narratives of social exclusion', *Deviant Behavior* 40(1), pp. 96–109.

8   Tumblr, 6 December 2019.

9   For more about this effect, known in psychology as the 'rejection–identification' model, see Chapter 6, note 23.

10   Mark Follman and Becca Andrews, 'How Columbine spawned dozens of copycats', *Mother Jones*, 5 October 2015. Available at http://www.motherjones.com/politics/2015/10/columbine-effect-mass-shootings-copycat-data.

11 Peter Langman (2018), 'Role models, contagions, and copycats: an exploration of the influence of prior killers on subsequent attacks', available at www.schoolshooters.info.

12 Anders Breivik murdered 77 people in two attacks in Norway on 22 July 2011, 69 of them at a young people's summer camp.

13 This comment was posted on 8chan on 27 March 2019, twelve days after the massacre.

14 Graham Macklin and Tore Bjørgo (2021), 'Breivik's long shadow? The impact of the July 22, 2011 attacks on the modus operandi of extreme-right lone actor terrorists', *Perspectives on Terrorism* 15(3), pp. 14–36. Several researchers have pointed out that school shootings and politically-inspired mass killings have much in common: see Sandberg et al. (2014); and Nils Böckler et al. (2018), 'Shootings', *Violence and Gender* 5(2), pp. 70–80.

15 Figures from the Anti-Defamation League, New York, www.adl.org.

16 The link between media coverage of suicides and the suicide rate is well established. See Daniel Ownby and Wesley Routon (2020), 'Tragedy following tragedies: estimating the copycat effect of media-covered suicide in the age of digital news', *The American Economist* 65(2), pp. 312–29.

17 It's fortunate that there is only a weak link between thought and action: psychological studies have revealed that the vast majority of us fantasize about killing someone at one time or another. For example, in a study at the University of Texas, 91 per cent of male and 76 per cent of female college students reported having had at least one homicidal thought: Joshua Duntley (2005), 'Homicidal ideations', PhD dissertation, University of Texas, available at https://repositories.lib.utexas.edu/bitstream/handle/2152/1897/duntleyj48072.pdf.

For further insights into the psychological differences between extremist thought and extremist action, see Clark McCauley and Sophia Moskalenko (2016), and Peter Neumann (2013).

18 Most research on the links between language and aggression and the predictive power of linguistic analysis has focused on extremist groups rather than school shooters or other 'lone actors'. See

James Pennebaker (2011), 'Using computer analyses to identify language style and aggressive intent: the secret life of function words', *Dynamics of Asymmetric Conflict* 4(2), pp. 92–102; and Lucian Conway III et al. (2011), 'The hidden implications of radical group rhetoric: integrative complexity and terrorism', *Dynamics of Asymmetric Conflict* 4(2), pp. 155–65.

19 For a deeper analysis of why it is unhelpful to describe terrorists like Tarrant, Breivik and the Columbine shooters as 'lone wolves', see Bart Schuurman et al. (2017), 'End of the lone wolf: the typology that should not have been', *Studies in Conflict and Terrorism* 42(8): 771–8.

20 See Lasse Lindekilde, Stefan Malthaner and Francis O'Connor (2019), 'Peripheral and embedded: relational patterns of lone-actor terrorist radicalization', *Dynamics of Asymmetric Conflict* (12)1, pp. 20–41; and Clark McCauley, Sophia Moskalenko and Benjamin Van Son (2013), 'Characteristics of lone-wolf violent offenders: a comparison of school attackers and assassins', *Perspectives on Terrorism* 7(1), pp. 4–24.

21 This is true for male serial killers, who make up the vast majority; female serial killers tend to kill people close to them.

22 Harold Schechter, *Deviant: The shocking true story of Ed Gein, the original Psycho* (Pocket Books, 1989), p. 238.

23 Some of these details first appeared in Michael Bond, 'Why are we eternally fascinated by serial killers?', *BBC Future*, 31 March 2016, available here: https://www.bbc.com/future/article/20160331-why-are-we-eternally-fascinated-by-serial-killers.

24 These items were all available for sale on 15 September 2021.

Index

Page numbers in **bold** indicate figures.

INDEX

INDEX

INDEX

INDEX